25 SKI TOURS IN NEW HAMPSHIRE

From the White Mountains to the Sea

Roioli Schweiker

A 25 SKI TOURS™ BOOK

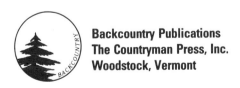
Backcountry Publications
The Countryman Press, Inc.
Woodstock, Vermont

An Invitation to the Reader —

With time, trails may be rerouted and signs and landmarks altered. If you find that changes have occurred on the routes described in this book, please let the author and publisher know so that corrections may be made in future editions. Other comments and suggestions are also welcome. Address all correspondence to:

Editor, *25 Ski Tours*™
Backcountry Publications
P.O. Box 175
Woodstock, VT 05091

Library of Congress Cataloging-in-Publication Data
Schweiker, Roioli.
    25 ski tours in New Hampshire : from the White Mountains to the sea / Roioli Schweiker.
        p. cm. — (A 25 ski tours book)
      ISBN 0-88150-114-X (pbk.) : $8.95
      1. Skis and skiing—New Hampshire—Guide-books.   2. New Hampshire—
—Description and travel—1981—Guide-books.   I. Title.
II. Title: Twenty-five ski tours in New Hampshire.   III. Series.
GV854.5.N4S38 1988   88-28177
917.420443—dc19   CIP

Published by Backcountry Publications
A division of the Countryman Press, Inc.
Woodstock, VT 05091

Photographs by: Roioli Schweiker, Jim Lewis, Amelia Archibald, Jim Fielding, Viloya Schweiker Allured, Marcia Cassin, and Roy Schweiker

Cover photograph and photographs on pages 51, 75, and 109 by Dick Smith, Jackson ski touring.

Illustration on page 8 by V. Beck

Cover design by Virginia L. Scott
Layout by Richard Widhu
Maps by Richard Widhu, © 1988 by The Countryman Press, Inc.
Printed in the United States of America

ACKNOWLEDGMENTS

My heartfelt appreciation goes to these people who accompanied me along the way:

Amelia Archibald
Jim Fielding
Anna Hoehn
Jim Lewis
Roy Schweiker
Debi Giolito
Lucie Strayer
Jeanne Lewis
Nelson Perrin
JoAnn Miele

Thanks also to Eugene Daniell III who measured the trails: Jamie Marshall, my editor; and Dan Doan, Dave Hardy, and Jed Eliades who suggested trips.

The Rangers of the White Mountain National Forest and the New Hampshire Division of Parks and Recreation and the Division of Lands and Forests were helpful in providing information.

Special thanks to my son, Roy, who helped me check everything, and my husband, Robert, who held up my end of the household while I was busy having all the fun skiing.

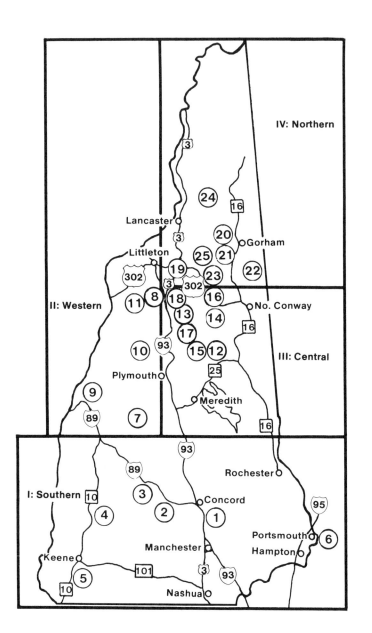

CONTENTS

Introduction   7

SOUTHERN   21
1. Bear Brook State Park   22
2. Elm Brook Park   27
3. Fox State Forest   31
4. Hubbard Hill   36
5. Kilburn Pond Ski Loop   41
6. Odiorne Point State Park   46

WESTERN   51
7. Cardigan   52
8. Franconia Notch   56
9. Mink Brook Trail   61
10. Three Ponds Loop   65
11. Tunnel Brook   70

CENTRAL   75
12. Flat Mountain Ponds   76
13. Greeley Ponds   81
14. Upper Nanamocomuck Ski Trail   84
15. Sandwich Notch   89
16. Sawyer River Road   94
17. Smarts Brook Area   98
18. Wilderness Trail/East Branch Trail   103

NORTHERN   109
19. Beaver Brook Ski Trails   110
20. Hayes Copp Ski Trail   115
21. Lowe's Bald Spot   119
22. Mountain Pond   125
23. Rocky Branch Trail   129
24. Willard Notch   132
25. Zealand Valley   136

Appendix: Cross-country ski areas   143

Vaulting is the easy way to get over a fallen tree.

INTRODUCTION

Winter is a beautiful season in northern New England. Each new snowfall creates a whole new world, even familiar areas becoming unrecognizable in a white frosted topping.

When I was a child, the coming of wnter meant anticipation of Christmas to my friends; to me the excitement was the first snowfall, and the next, and the next . . . And in those days all I knew to do was to walk in it, and make snowmen, and coast on a sled. How much more exciting to discover skiing, which enabled me to cover more ground enjoyably in search of winter beauty.

This is a "where to" and not a "how to" book on skiing. Discussions about ski equipment and technique are well covered in other publications. However, for people moving out from tracked skiing to wilderness skiing, a few suggestions may be in order.

Many of the trails described are maintained by volunteers —if at all—and then usually just for the hiking season. Blowdowns and fallen branches are not uncommon. Take a minute and toss aside anything small enough to handle easily. When a deadfall too large to move has blocked the trail, notify the administering organization. Parties who customarily ski on infrequently used trails sometimes carry small folding saws (the kind that resemble an oversize jackknife) to help dispose of such blockages.

Snow conditions are as they occur, not improved by grooming machines. Bridges are designed for hikers rather than skiers, in most cases, and approaches may be difficult. A good method for slowing down (see the photograph in Chapter 1) is to grasp the poles together with the upper hand, place the lower hand palm down on them with the fingers pointed toward the baskets, and drag them between your legs. Another is to drag the poles together on one side. If there is a curve, drag them on the inside of the turn.

As you ski along, watch for signs of animals. One of the most interesting is the track left by the snowshoe rabbit. If you don't know better, you may think the tracks are going in the opposite direction from what they actually are. The large prints of the hind feet come down forward of the offset smaller prints of the front feet as the rabbit vaults along. The pads are big and have furry webs that enable the rabbit to stay on top of the snow. Beagle dogs, which chase rabbits, have similar foot pads.

Deer—unlike rabbits—have small, sharp feet for their size. They sink deeper into the snow, making easily identifiable holes. Their hooves are divided into two parts and make a track the size of a child's palm. Deer pellets are the size of the last joint of the little finger, brown and earthy looking. Rabbit pellets have somewhat the same texture, but more resemble brown M&Ms.

Moose leave tracks similar to a deer, but larger — the size of a man's palm. Their droppings are correspondingly larger as well; they are currently popular, dried and varnished, as moose drop necklaces.

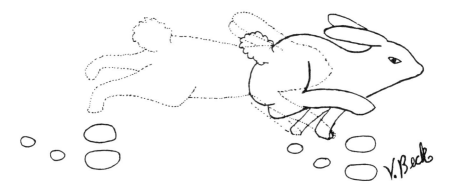

Keep in mind that the areas described in this book are not the exclusive preserve of skiers—snowmobiles, snowshoers, hikers, and dogs also use them. In some cases this makes the terrain more manageable; in others, less so. Make the best of it, smile, and, if necessary, go elsewhere. It is their outdoors, too.

Remember that much of the time you will be alone in the woods. In the event of an emergency there's no ski patrol to count on, nor any other assistance. Because of this, each party must be self-sufficient, in terms of both numbers and equipment.

Selecting a Tour

The trips in this book were selected not only to provide a diversity of location and terrain, but also because I happened to enjoy them. They represent only a fraction of the possibilities in New Hampshire.

Because ski trails tend to follow valleys instead of climbing to summits like hiking trails, views are less common. Two exceptions are Hubbard Hill (see Chapter 4 for information on how to use a compass to identify the peaks you see) and Lowe's Bald Spot. Many trips have ponds as major or alternate destinations; several lead to narrow notches.

The trips are arranged alphabetically within four sections. This, plus the information listing at the start of each chapter, allows for a quick selection of a suitable trip for the day.

SOUTHERN

Trips in the southern section lie south of Lake Winnipesaukee. Three are in New Hampshire State Parks, one in a New Hampshire State Forest, one in the area of a flood control dam, and one is administered by a conservation organization.

Traditionally, most of our state parks have been closed in the winter. But with the increasing focus on fitness recreation, more and more are starting to offer opportunities for winter recreation. In many cases this means snowmobiles, or multiple use. However, some do restrict certain roads or trails to skiers; in others, ski trails have been cut or are planned.

WESTERN

Trips in the western section lie west of I-93. Franconia Notch is a state park. The trails at Cardigan and Mink Brook are a combination of pre-existing trails, old roads, and trails cut especially for skiing. Three Ponds Loop and Tunnel Brook follow hiking trails, partially on old roads, in the southwestern corner of the White Mountain National Forest. The trail in Franconia Notch, although paralleling the Interstate much of the way, offers a succession of outstanding views of the Old Man of the Mountain and the Notch's other scenic attractions.

CENTRAL

The trips in central New Hampshire lie between the lakes and the southern end of the great notches, an area that has few public roads at all, and even fewer that are plowed in winter. Most of the land belonged to the great logging barons until well into the 20th century, and their railroads, skid roads, towns, and services were almost its only life for more than 50 years. Now, almost all of this land lies within the White Mountain National Forest.

The Kancamagus Highway, which runs east-west across the area, was opened in 1959, and has only been open in winter since the late 1960s. Today, there is still no through north-south road. The Sandwich Notch, Tripoli, and Bear Notch roads are closed by snow each winter.

Perhaps the most notable feature of the White Mountain

ski trips is the network of old logging railroads. Eight of
the trips (four each in the Central and Northern sections)
occur at least partially on old railroad grades—almost
every valley had its own railroad at one time. For more information on the old railroads, see C. Francis Belcher's
Logging Railroads of the White Mountains (Appalachian
Mountain Club, Boston, 1980).

A major drawback to using old logging railroads as ski
routes is that originally they crossed rivers back and forth
on trestles, all but one of which are now missing from
flood, fire, collapse or removal. Hiking trails generally stay
on one side of the river, but these can be difficult to ski.
Missing culverts and minor erosion also cause dips in the
trail. The tours in this section have been designed to take
advantage of the old railroad beds, while avoiding their
most difficult spots.

NORTHERN

The remaining trips are in the northern half of the White
Mountains and are all within the National Forest. Much of
the touring is on logging roads and unplowed back roads,
but hiking trails, ski trails and old railroad beds are also used.

To a large extent, the creation of the White Mountain
National Forest was a reaction to the expansion of the
logging railroads, whose abandoned roadbeds we skiers
enjoy today. By the late 1800s there was growing concern
about the railroads, wasteful logging practices, and des-
tructive forest fires, caused, or at least exacerbated by
them. The Society for the Protection of New Hampshire
Forests was formed in 1901. Its chief executive officer,
Philip Ayers, campaigned for a federal forest reserve, ar-
guing that the White Mountains were a national treasure.
Passage by the U.S. Congress of the Weeks Act in 1911
opened the way for the purchase of the timberlands and
the establishment of the White Mountain National Forest as
a multi-use working forest. The Wilderness Areas were

formed beginning in 1964 to improve protection and reduce man's impact on selected areas of the forest.

ADDITIONAL SKIING

This book provides an introduction to some of the best backcountry ski touring in New Hampshire, but the state offers many more excellent ski-touring opportunities. As mentioned above, most of the New Hampshire State Parks are opening new and improved winter recreational opportunities, including cross-country ski trails. The White Mountain National Forest has built many such trails, some of which are partially groomed. The Army Corps of Engineers provides recreational areas at flood control dams, as feasible.

Some back roads are unplowed in winter and make good ski-touring routes. Many hiking trails, especially in valleys, are suitable for skiing, although hiker traffic may make the surface unsuitable.

Towns often provide skiing opportunities for their residents at municipal golf courses, conservation areas and parks. Organizations such as the Audubon Society and the Forest Society allow skiing on their property.

A list of cross-country ski centers is in the Appendix. These centers charge a fee for trail use, offer rentals and instruction, and their snowmaking and grooming often allows skiing when natural snow cover is sparse.

Maps

These tour descriptions are intended to stand alone. However, the Appalachian Mountain Club, the DeLorme Publishing Company, and the United States Geological Survey all publish topographical maps of the White Mountains with some of the trails marked on them. DeLorme's *Trail Map and Guide to the White Mountain National Forest* is particularly helpful. The state parks, the U.S. Forest Service, and the Society for the Protection of New Hampshire Forests print maps of their ski trails, usually without contour lines.

Any maps that would be useful in addition to the sketch maps included with each chapter are listed at the beginning of the tour. A list of addresses for maps and information is at the end of this section. The following is a list of abbreviations used in the map listings:

USGS – United States Geological Survey
AMC – Appalachian Mountain Club
USFS – United States Forest Service
SPNHF – Society for the Protection of New Hampshire Forests
DeLorme – Trail Map and Guide to the White Mountain National Forest

The elevation profiles which accompany the maps in this book were not surveyed but are included to give a feeling for the rise and fall of the tours. However, at their scale of one-half inch to the mile horizontally and one-sixteenth inch to 100 feet vertically, small dips and climbs don't show. In all cases, the trip starts at the left and moves to the right.

Sources of Maps and Other Information

New Hampshire Division of Parks and Recreation, 105 Loudon Road, Concord, NH 03301 (603-271-3556)

New Hampshire Division of Forests and Lands, Box 856, Concord, NH 03301 (603-271-2214)

Society for the Protection of New Hampshire Forests, 54 Portsmouth St., Concord, NH 03301 (603-224-9945)

Appalachian Mountain Club, Pinkham Notch, Box 258, Gorham, NH 03581 (603-466-2727) or 5 Joy St., Boston, MA 02108 (617-523-0636)

DeLorme Publishing Co., Box 298-88, Freeport, ME 04032 (207-865-4171)

United States Geological Survey, Map Distribution Branch, Box 25286, Denver Federal Center, Denver, Colorado 80225 (303-236-7477)

United States Forest Service, White Mountain National Forest, 719 Main St., Laconia, NH (603-524-6450)

Ranger District offices:
Saco—at east end of Kancamagus Highway at NH-16, Conway (603-447-5448)

Pemigewasset—on NH-175 a mile north of the bridge in Plymouth (603-563-1310)

Ammonoosuc—1 mile north of US-3 at "Five Corners," which is 5 miles west of Twin Mountain (603-869-2626)

Androscoggin—on NH-16 south of Gorham (603-466-2713)

Driving Directions

The official New Hampshire road map, which can be obtained free from all state rest areas, is the basic source for driving directions. All towns and numbered highways given as starting points appear on it, as well as state parks, historic landmarks, and other tourist attractions.

Begin by locating the town mentioned in the directions in the index and finding it on the map. This will allow you to plan a route from your home or rendezvous location to the starting point. From there, follow the driving directions.

The DeLorme *New Hampshire Atlas and Gazetteer,* a blue and green book measuring 11 x 15 inches, is widely available in bookstores and sporting goods stores. Its maps show all public back roads in the state and are invaluable for anyone who ventures off the numbered highways.

Trip Descriptions

All these trips are one-way descriptions only. Where appropriate, a specific turn or difficult spot that requires special care on the return is mentioned. Loops are described in what I considered the better direction. With the exception of specially designated "one-way" trails, however, the loops may be started from either end.

In some cases, alternate or additional trips in the area are also described.

Trail Data

Distance is given in miles. The one-way mileage is given on trips where you return the same way. On loops the total loop distance from the car to the return is given.

Difficulty is divided into four categories.
   Minimal: Route is nearly level, surface smooth, streams and dips well bridged.
   Easy: Surface mostly smooth, gradient gentle. Some snowplowing and/or sidestepping may be required.
   Moderate: Steeper and/or narrower trail, requiring good control by snowplowing or other braking technique. Streams generally unbridged and may be awkward to cross. (See chapter 12 for hints on herringboning and sidestepping on steep, narrow trails.)
   Difficult: Just what it says! Steep narrow trails requiring considerable skiing ability to negotiate safely.

Surfaces range from unplowed paved roads to steep, rocky hiking trails.

Time is not specified for the trips. Travel in winter is too dependent on snow conditions. After a few trips you will learn to estimate your own time. Surface makes a great difference—travel is faster on a graded road than a hiking trail.

Trailhead Notes and Cautions

Most of these tours do not come with plowed, sanded parking lots. Whatever parking areas do exist tend to be the last places plowed. When the snow is deep, you may have difficulty finding off-road parking, or you may return from a tour to find your car plowed in.

Therefore you should be prepared to dig your car out or even occasionally to dig yourself a parking space. If you find a snowbank blocking off-road parking space, it is sometimes possible to dig a car-sized hole perpendicularly into the bank. Park far enough in to be safe if the plow goes by.

To be prepared for these possibilities, you should have a good shovel in the car, a strong brush and ice scraper, and a container of sand. (*Dry* sand can be carried in a cola bottle and will not freeze.) A tow rope, jumper cables, mud hooks, and a carburetor de-icer are helpful to have along. Old newspapers stuffed inside a plastic garbage bag provide a dry spot for working on tires or putting on chains. Work gloves protect the hands.

You would be wise also to bring a few old blankets, dry clothes, and emergency food—to sustain you in the unlikely event you get stranded in your car. Carry a spare key, preferably hidden outside the car.

DO NOT LEAVE ANY VALUABLES AT ALL IN YOUR CAR! Leave purses and overstuffed wallets at home. Take only the cash and credit cards you will need in a small wallet, and carry it in your pocket.

Courtesy on the Trail

Just because others are not thoughtful is no reason you should not be! Leave no litter about, and this includes little candy wrappers and twist ties.

Do not remove your skis for stream crossings and dips unless the rocks are bare, or the track frozen hard. If you do choose to walk a difficult spot, don't mess up the tracks for more skillful skiers. Walk out of the tracks, or better yet, make your own route. On ski trails, or where it would cause problems for others, fill in sitzmarks.

Few of these trails come with outhouses. Where you have a need, but not a facility, get well off the trail. Since your deposit will be there until the thaw, consider where it is going to be washed to, and try not to pollute running water. Toilet paper is still going to make a mess in the spring, and leaves are sparse at this time of year. If you don't wish to carry the used paper with you in a plastic bag, consider the use of snowballs. They are very refreshing.

Breaking trail.

On a one-lane road, upbound automobiles and horse-drawn wagons have the right of way; however with skiers, the downhill skier has the right of way. You should also move off the trail for snowmobiles since you can hear them coming, but they can't know that you are around a blind curve.

Food

Take a sufficient quantity of the type of food that survives well in the cold. If you are trying to lose weight, cut down on dinner, not breakfast and lunch. Drink at least as much liquid as usual—more if exercising strenuously—to avoid dehydration. A canteen of hot water with some lemonade powder wrapped in newspaper and your spare sweater, will not freeze. Be sure the cap is on tight.

It isn't possible to have too many cookies! They are great for making friends with people, as well as animals and birds.

Clothing

Color coordinated ski-touring outfits are attractive, but they leave little margin for error. If you are going far off the highway, or if the weather is cold, consider wearing, or at least carrying, something more appropriate for winter conditions. Lots of layers are the way to go, so you can adjust your clothing to the amount of exercise, temperature, and wind.

Gaiters should be worn when the snow is fluffy to prevent it from getting into your boots. Gaiters also help keep your feet warm.

Shell mittens, with a water repellant outer cover and wool mittens inside, are much more practical than gloves. The inner mittens can be removed when hot or for drying at home. Dry ones can be exchanged when necessary. A mountaineering style parka is also recommended. A knit ski hat will add as much warmth as another sweater, maybe more.

Stream Crossings

Most of the streams mentioned can be crossed on snow bridges. Unless you are crossing on bare rocks, keep your skis on to distribute your weight as widely as possible. Do not probe the snow, as it may weaken a bridge that might otherwise have held. If you must do so, use a stick instead of a ski pole, to make a smaller hole.

The best way to cross a steep dip is to ski it diagonally. Failing this, sidestep rather than herringbone; you are less likely to slide back into the water.

Should your skis get wet, take them off and dry them immediately, rewaxing if necessary. Should a foot get wet, change to dry socks. Put a plastic bread bag over the socks to keep them from the wet boot. If there is a shortage of dry socks, put on only one dry sock next to the foot, and put the plastic bag between it and the outside wet sock, wrung out.

Safety

The U.S. Forest Service and the U.S. Ski Association put out an excellent booklet, *Winter Recreation Safety Guide,* available from your local ranger. Since it is geared to the whole country, some things like avalanche safety are irrelevant on these trails. Still, it has much good advice.

Avoid long loop trips if you are inexperienced, the weather is bad, or if it is early in the season, when you are not in shape and days are short.

If you are having difficulty on a loop, unless you are *sure* you are *much* more than halfway, return the way you came. At least you know what the trail is like, and can find it in adverse conditions.

Carry emergency equipment suitable for the trip. Accidents happen even half a mile from the road!

On narrow, ungraded trails, don't use the loops on your poles. Catching the basket on a stub can lead to an abrupt, jarring halt—or worse.

Carry wax, even if you have waxless skis; it is useful on steep climbs, in warm weather, or after immersion.

Listen to the weather forecast, but don't believe it too seriously. I have shoveled a lot of "partly cloudy" off my driveway.

Map Legend

- 𝝜 **Appalachian Trail**
- ⓟ **Parking**
- — — — **Main Trail**
- • • • • • • **Side Trail**
- ▲ **Mountain**
- ◀ **Direction of Travel**
- ⚠ **Campground**
- ■ **Shelter**
- ▬▬▬ ▬ ▬ ▬ **Road**
- ◀ **Reverse Direction of Travel**
- ⇐ **View**

SOUTHERN

1 BEAR BROOK STATE PARK

Allenstown

	Long Loop	Short Loop	Road/Trail
Distance:	7.5-mile loop	5-mile loop	4.8-mile loop
Difficulty:	moderate/difficult	moderate/easy	easy/moderate
Surface:	ski trail	ski trail/logging road	road

Maps: USGS Suncook 15', Bear Brook State Park

Bear Brook State Park has a rolling terrain, cut by small brooks and a few lakes. Because the elevation difference on the ski trail is only 200 feet, no profile is given. This doesn't mean that there are no hills, only that you reuse the same elevation difference, going up and down.

The park has a network of roads that are unplowed and open to all forms of winter recreation: snowmobiles, skiers, ATVs, dog sleds. Two interconnected loop trails are restricted to cross-country skiers; the surface on the long loop is rough, and requires good snow cover to make enjoyable skiing.

On the map, the numbers circled are the signed road junctions. The letters XC plus a number are the ski trail junctions, either with the road or another ski trail.

Driving Directions

From NH-28 at the north side of Allenstown, just south of the Suncook River bridge, turn east toward Deerfield at the sign to Bear Brook State Park. Go 3.2 miles, passing the snowmobile parking area on the right at 0.7 mile, and bearing right at intersections.

Turn right at the sign for cross-country ski parking. Drive down the hill, across the bridge, and up the other side. Turn right down to the large parking lot.

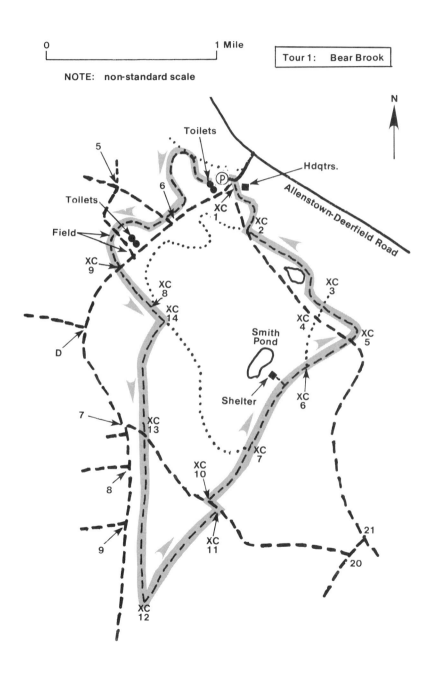

Long Loop

The trail starts just to the right of the outhouses, and may be hard to see if the snowbanks in the parking lot are particularly high. It runs through the woods a short way, then comes out on an old road, which it follows left. Watch for the left turn off of the road.

Narrow and rough, the trail climbs steeply and switchbacks past a small quarry to the top of the rise. It drops and crosses a snowmobiled road, bears right at a trail junction and, after about one and a half miles, comes out into an open field. Outhouses are located in the near edge of the woods, to the left. Turn left and cross the field to the road. XC-9 is across the road just before an open marsh.

Enter the woods on an old road. Pass a trail to the left at XC-8 and a half mile from the field turn right at XC-14. Continue along, crossing a couple of brooks, and circle up to the road at XC-13. After crossing the road here, you'll find the next mile-long southward leg to be the roughest part of the trip. It circles along a sidehill among medium-sized rocks, where a deep snow cover is needed to make the skiing pleasant. At XC-12 the trail turns sharply back left on an old road. Here the going is easier, trending somewhat downward.

At XC-11 turn left on the road for a short way to XC-10 where you turn right, soon crossing a small bridge. Most of this section is easy going. Take a well-traveled left to the shelter on Smith Pond—within sight of the trail—attractively situated on a small rise.

Back on the trail, continue on to XC-6, where you take a right and soon cross the road at XC-5. Now in the woods, a narrow trail climbs a little and drops down to a picnic area on a small pond that is circled on the far side from the road. Climb a little more, and then follow a steep downgrade for the last half mile to the start.

Short Loop

More of this trip is on old roads than the long loop. The short loop is less rough and requires slightly less snow. There are a number of wet spots, however, which can give trouble in warm weather.

Begin by backtracking up the road to the parking lot. Cross the road and take the trail that leads between the road and the buildings. In a quarter mile at XC-2, turn right and cross the road. Climb up the hill in sweeping switchbacks to XC-8, which is one and eight tenths of a mile from the start. Turn left to another old road, and left again at XC-14. Ski slightly downhill crossing some wet areas. At XC-7 turn left and follow the last portion of the long loop trip description.

Slowing down on a hill past an obstruction.

Road/Ski Trail Loop

This trip is even easier than the other two loops, provided the snow is in good condition. Keep in mind that the road may be icy due to heavy usage.

Go back up the hill from the parking area and take the road to the right. Continue climbing up the hill past the big field on the right. (The road climbs a hundred feet more than the ski trail in this area). At Junction 7 turn left. The road trends downhill, giving a good run. At XC-10, turn left on the ski trail, and follow it past the Smith Pond shelter. At XC-6 take the left, for a short downhill run, and turn left on the road, which you follow back to the start.

ELM BROOK PARK

Hopkinton

	1.	**2.**
Distance:	1 mile one way	1¾ mile each way
Difficulty:	minimal	minimal
Surface:	graded	graded

Map: USGS Hopkinton 7½'

For an easy ski trip near population centers and a main highway, try Elm Brook Park, administered by the Army Corps of Engineers. Those who dislike the sight or sound of snowmobiles might prefer to stay away, but although there were some in the distance one sunny Saturday, I actually met only three skiers and one snowmobile on the trip described.

After severe damage to bridges and property from several floods, particularly that of 1936, the U.S. government built several large flood control reservoirs in New Hampshire. One of the largest is in Hopkinton and Weare, completed in 1962, which contains 7,342 acres of land and 650 acres of water at normal times. During floods, the project is designed to pond water to reduce downsteam damage. It includes an earth dam at West Hopkinton, which serves as the Route 127 crossing of the Contoocook River, and another dam at East Weare on the North Branch of the Piscataquog River. Rather than being in a steep-sided valley like many flood control projects, the Hopkinton-Everett Reservoir is located in a relatively flat area, so a number of long dikes were necessary to prevent water from spilling out the sides of the valley. This tour travels along the tops of two of these dikes, which are water level flat.

Driving Directions

To reach the park, take I-89 to Exit 6, and take Route 127

South. After 1.2 miles, turn left at the park sign, proceed up a short hill, turn sharp right, and descend. The parking lot to the left, just before the gate, is usually plowed.

The Tour

For the first part of the tour, walk about a hundred yards back up the road you just came in. A gated road to the left leads off as straight as an arrow: this is the first dike. The land to the left is within the reservoir, while that to the right is protected by the dike. DO NOT SKI DOWN THE SIDE OF THE DIKE, as the snow hides large boulders used for rip-rap, and traversing them is not only hazardous but possibly illegal. It is just less than a mile across the dike, and on the other side you can continue along the road to an open area. Straight ahead is a good view of the Hopkinton Dam. The building to the right across the field is the project manager's office, usually closed on weekends. You can return to the parking lot by the same route, for a scenic and easy 2 miles.

For the next part of the tour, continue down the main entrance road past the gate. If the road is plowed or icy, carry your skis. Pass a picnic shelter on a knoll to the right, and start down the hill. About 200 yards from the parking lot, turn left on a level, gated service road. (The main road straight ahead continues to the summer picnic area and boat launch.) The service road circles along the contour of the land, with a minimum of gradient. At about half a mile, this road crosses another road, and soon comes out into a large open area, with views to the right across Elm Brook Marsh. About a mile from the parking area, the road climbs moderately and then steeply to the top of another dike. Relax, this hill is short enough to walk or sidestep if necessary. At the top of the dike, turn left for a quick side trip to the emergency spillway. The water will flow down this channel when the reservoir is full to capacity; imagine what the surrounding countryside looked like in April 1987 when the water was nearly up to this point.

Now, turn around and head across the dike. This dike is curved, and the surrounding area is more wooded. Look down to the left, and perhaps you will see a beaver pond and beaver house. This dike is only three-quarters of a mile long, and the road ends just beyond. The traffic you hear in the woods ahead is on I-89. Your return is by the same route.

There is plenty of other skiing available in the park, but as of this writing there are no marked trails. Avoid the sides of

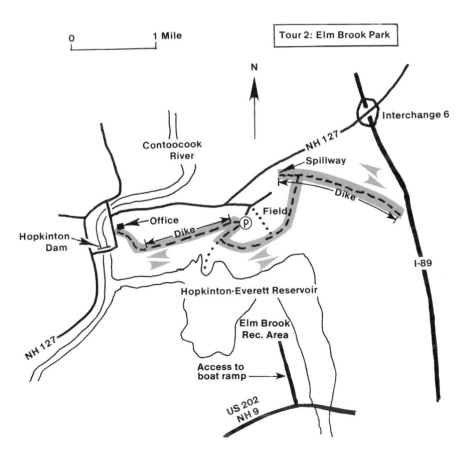

the dikes and canals, and do not venture onto the ice, as water levels may fluctuate drastically due to reservoir operations. For more information, contact the Project Manager at 746-3601 on weekdays.

A bird on the pole is worth....

FOX STATE FOREST

	Ridge Trail	**Hurricane/Proctor Roads**
Distance:	5-mile loop	3¾-mile loop
Difficulty:	moderate/difficult	easy/moderate
Surface:	hiking trail	gravel road

Maps: Fox State Forest Map, USGS Hillsborough 15

The trip described here in the Caroline Fox Research and Demonstration Forest is more of a forest experience that can be enjoyed on skis, rather than a ski trip. The site has been studied since 1932. Various species have been planted and results of forest management practices observed. Some of the trees have name labels on them.

Although the Ridge Trail is neither excessively long nor excessively steep, it is designed as a minimally marked, low-impact hiking trail. Both a deep base and good surface conditions are needed. There are few directional signs, and while the blazes on the trees are sufficient to follow, they require careful and continuous attention. Don't forget your compass. If backtracking does not locate the proper route, you can follow a road or major trail east and north back to the main road.

Driving Directions
From the blinking light in the center of Hillsborough, take the road north; a sign points to "Fox Forest." The State Forest Headquarters, with a plowed parking area, is 1.9 miles on the right.

Ridge Trail Loop
The Ridge Trail, which is blazed with red-on-white-painted vertical rectangles, starts across the road from the parking

area, just north of the entrance where a sign reads, "to Hurricane Road." The area is a network of trails, none of the junctions are marked; follow your blazes carefully.

The trail runs downhill and up at a gentle grade to Hurricane Road. Turn left, then continue straight where the road bears left. Soon there will be a sign to a viewpoint called the Ledges, which looks back across the valley to the start. Where the more heavily used trail bears right downhill into the Black Gum Swamp, continue ahead.

(A side trip to the swamp is only a hundred yards. The large tree with bark like a lumpy alligator, just west of the sign, is the aforementioned black gum. The swamp itself is a kettlehole, formed when the glacier left a huge block of ice that in turn left a depression in the debris when it melted and formed a pond without an outlet. The area subsequently filled in with vegetation.)

Back on the Ridge Trail, keep sharp right where the red-slash trail goes ahead. A short, steep drop is followed by a gentle uphill back to Hurricane Road. Turn right on the road, then right again, uphill, where the road bears left down to a "T" intersection. This next section climbs slightly and crosses another road at a blue cornerpost. After a short, steep chute, pass an open area on the left, and climb gently to a large white oak tree.

This 60-foot tree, with a circumference of 11 feet, 6 inches, is one of the largest trees in the area. Because it grew at the edge of a field, its branches spread widely outward, instead of growing tall and thin as trees do in a forest. The timbers in the lower branches are probably the remains of a hunter's deer stand. Deer feed in fields instead of deep woods, and hunters often climb trees to give themselves an inconspicuous vantage point.

The blue blazes mark the boundary of Fox Forest, and the

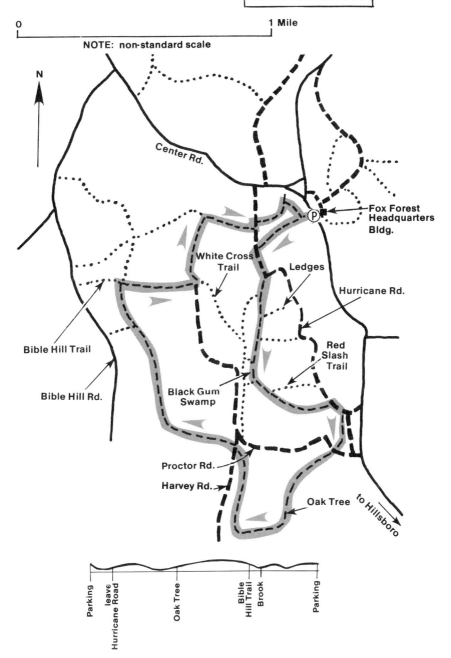

Tour 3: Fox State Forest

0   1 Mile

NOTE: non-standard scale

N

Center Rd.

Fox Forest
Headquarters
Bldg.

White Cross
Trail

Ledges

Hurricane Rd.

Bible Hill Trail

Red
Slash
Trail

Bible Hill Rd.

Black Gum
Swamp

Proctor Rd.

Harvey Rd.

Oak Tree

to Hillsboro

Parking

leave
Hurricane Road

Oak Tree

Bible
Hill Trail

Brook

Parking

trail turns right, westward, along them. A power line parallels the boundary, and walking out to its clearing offers a minor view of local hills.

The Ridge Trail continues along the boundary, falling steeply down to a brook and then up and down, bearing right along a stone wall with a wire fence.

Cross Harvey Road and continue west toward Bible Hill Road, gradually bearing north. Beyond, where it leaves the stone wall, the trail bears right downhill in the pines. On the left some large rocks look like a snow-covered Alpine village; just beyond is the junction with the Bible Hill Trail.

Switchback east and down to a brook. Another trail turns left and follows the brook; the Ridge Trail climbs steeply up the ridge. At the top, turn left on the road, and left again on the White Cross Trail. The route runs down to a wet area where there is extensive beaver activity. Turn right on the road, which leads along the side of the hill back to Hurricane Road. The Ridge Trail jogs left on the road across the brook, then in 100 feet turns right across a wet area, passes the blue-blazed boundary, and soon comes out on the plowed road. Within sight of the road, you can bear right on a trail blazed with white spots that follows the road east to the trail where you started. Turn left, the road is within sight.

Hurricane/Proctor Roads

Start as described on the Ridge Trail, but continue on Hurricane Road, downhill to the low point at the junction of Proctor Road. Return on Proctor Road to the White Cross Trail. Go left on the White Cross Trail where it coincides with the Ridge Trail. Keep right on the Ridge Trail back to Hurricane Road. Turn right, then left on the Ridge Trail, the way you came in.

The loop on the road will be heavily snowmobiled, and it

runs uphill and down. However it is easier to ski, and much easier to follow, than the Ridge Trail. It can also be used as a short cut/escape route for people who find the Ridge Trail not to their liking.

Additional Skiing
On the east side of the road there are unplowed roads that can also be skied.

The big oak tree.

HUBBARD HILL

Stoddard

	Hubbard Hill	Jackson Hill	Pitcher Mt.
Distance:	2.1 miles each way	3.5-mile loop	0.3 mile each way
Difficulty:	moderate	difficult	difficult
Surface:	graded road	road/trail	trail

Map: SPNHF Greenway

The basic trip to Hubbard Hill rolls up and down, giving fairly easy ascents and descents, in both directions. The trip to Jackson Hill is scenic, but it is skiable only for experts in good snow conditions. The area is usually snowmobiled.

The route crosses, and in places coincides with, the Monadnock-Sunapee Greenway, a long-distance trail that was built in 1976 under the auspices of the Society for the Protection of New Hampshire Forests. The trail runs from Mt. Monadnock, 50 miles north to Mt. Sunapee, in general follwing the divide between the Connecticut and Merrimack watersheds. The original trail was cleared and marked with vertical 2-inch by 6-inch painted white rectangles; a number of relocations have been made to move it from roads and improve the route. Five campsites allow a longer trip that can be extended even further thanks to the Metacomet-Monadnock Trail, which travels south to Long Island Sound.

Driving Directions

The Monadnock-Sunapee Greenway crosses NH-123 near the height-of-land west of the town of Stoddard, and between NH-10 on the west and NH-9 on the east. The fire tower on Pitcher Mountain is visible for some distance, and it and the parking are on the north side of NH-123, approximately 1.8 miles west of Stoddard.

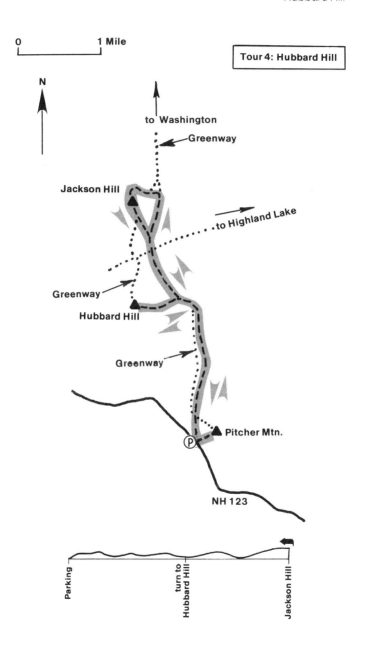

Hubbard Hill

The ski trail to Hubbard Hill starts on the left-hand road, which climbs and drops along a wide flatish ridge. The entire trip is exposed to the sun and wind. Meanwhile, the Greenway starts by climbing to the summit of Pitcher Mountain, then goes down the far side to the road on which you are skiing. It crosses to the left-hand side, and eventually comes back to the road.

After the third hill, a road leads left, with the Greenway and a sign to Hubbard Hill. Dip down, cross a private road, and continue up to a gate a tenth of a mile ahead, where there is the start of an open area with blueberry bushes. The road crosses this section to a higher point at the far end, with good views in all directions. Pitcher Mountain stands out to the southeast. The Greenway continues ahead as a trail.

Jackson Hill

Return to the last junction. The skiing on to Jackson Hill is considerably more difficult, as the grades are steeper and the road/trail narrower. If snow conditions are good, though, Jackson Hill is worth the trip. On the other hand, if snow conditions are terrible, it is usually because the road has been snowmobiled and is packed and icy. While I am strenuously opposed to people taking ski trails that are too difficult for them, and then walking and ruining the trail for other, more competent skiers, icy snowmobile tracks are another matter. Carrying skis on the steeper parts may be necessary.

If you elect to continue, stay in control on the downhills, which become very steep in places. In the next col is a 4-way junction: the right leads to Barden Pond and Highland Lake, the left is less obvious and unmarked. Ahead leads to Jackson Hill. Almost immediately is a fork where the left is a *very steep* trail to Jackson Hill. Take the right fork. This road climbs steeply to the col between the summits of

Jackson Hill and drops equally steeply on the other side. At the bottom of the steep grade is a beaver pond on the left. The Greenway returns to the road on the far side of the pond, circling high enough to keep the footway dry, and continues ahead down the road to Washington. You want to take a left on the Greenway, following the white-painted rectangles. The trail is narrow, lined with spruce trees, and climbs moderately to the summit of Jackson Hill.

Jackson Hill has a 360° view, with many surrounding mountains visible. The best way to identify these is to bring a state map along. If the wind is not too strong, spread out your space blanket or sit-upon, and put the map open at the southern part of the state on it.

A compass will be helpful to orient the map. The declination in this area is 14° west, so subtract 14° from 360° and point the north needle at 346°. If you don't know what declination is, and don't want to learn, just forget it. Using the compass uncorrected is better than not using a compass at all

I think of the magnetic pole as a great big magnet sitting up in northern Canada that attracts the compass needle.

That has to be Mt. Monadnock!

Therefore, the needle will point west of north in the northeast, and east of north in the west. Topographic and other large-scale, accurate maps come with the declination marked on them, usually near the compass arrow.

The declination for the area covered by these ski trips, and where I usually hike, ranges from 14° in southwest New Hampshire to 17° in the northern White Mountains. Since most people can't use a compass accurately within 5° to 10°, this difference is not that significant. I tape a mark on the face of my compass corresponding to 15½° (i.e. 344½°). Then I just point my needle at the mark.

To orient the map, lay the compass on the map. Turn the map until the top (or whatever other direction is so marked) is north according to the compass.

To identify a mountain: Take a couple of small sticks. Stand one on end at the place on the map where you are. (Pitcher Mountain is marked on the New Hampshire map. Jackson Hill is in a direct line northwest toward the west side of Ashuelot Pond, just south of the county line.) Sight your mountain over the top of the first stick using the second stick. Place the second stick on the map and look for the mountain shown in that area.

The easier way to return is the way you came. The hill down the other side of Jackson Hill is steeper, narrower, and only marginally skiable by experts under the right conditions. If you choose to do it, take the Greenway south. Where it turns right, stay on the road, and return to the place where you took the right just above the 4-way intersection.

Pitcher Mountain

From the parking area, the right-hand trail leads to the fire tower on Pitcher Mountain. If snow conditions are too poor to ski, the trail is probably sufficiently well-packed to walk up. Enjoy the view, and return to the parking lot.

KILBURN POND SKI LOOP

Pisgah State Park, Hinsdale/Winchester

	Kilburn Loop	**Mt. Pisgah**
Distance:	6.0-mile loop	2.2-mile roundtrip
Difficulty:	moderate	difficult
Surface:	road/trail	hiking trail

Maps: Pisgah State Park Map, USGS Keene 15′

Pisgah State Park in the southwestern part of New Hampshire is less well-known and developed than many of the state's other parks. Many new trails are presently under construction, but not in time to be included in this book.

The loop around Kilburn Pond is restricted to skiing, and is very attractive. Its chief drawback is that the start is near the highest point, so the return is almost all uphill. Although the loop was originally a hiking trail, all stream bridges are designed for crossing on skis.

Driving Directions

The ski-touring access to Pisgah State Park is from NH-63, 4.5 miles south of NH-9 and 4 miles north of NH-119. A small plowed area is on the east side of the road, marked by a sign on a tree on the far side, easy to miss.

Kilburn Pond Loop

From the parking area the route follows an old woods road, climbing gently and then steeply to the park boundary. From there, drop a while to the start of the Kilburn Ski Loop, 0.7 mile from the parking area.

There is a difference of opinion as to the direction to do the loop. The park recommends clockwise, which gives the steeper grades downhill in the morning, and the long, gentle upgrade in the afternoon. The friend who recommended the trip, suggested counterclockwise (which is the way it is described) as this gives just the opposite, which I prefer.

Bear right at the Kilburn Loop junction. The trail goes up and down along the shore of Kilburn Pond, a public water supply. Enjoy the views of the pond from here, as it is not visible from the east side of the loop. Periodic wet spots on the trail require attention to maintain dry skis. Skiers wanting an easy trip can go as far as Kilburn Pond and return.

The ski trail leaves the lakeside and climbs gently along the side of the hill, looking down on a marsh. The obligatory aisle through little evergreens is here lined with hemlocks instead of the spruces found in the northern woods. This is also about the northern boundary of mountain laurel; on the frigid winter day we visited, the leaves were curled back to compress the stomata on the underside and preserve moisture, and it looked like it wished it had gone south for the winter.

A "caution" sign warns of a steep hill; at the bottom there's a brook with a nice plank bridge across it. The trail sign warns "more difficult" as you go over a little rise and drop awkwardly to another bridge. You may wish to sidestep down to these bridges. This is the low point of the trip.

The trail then turns left and starts the long climb back up at a gentle to moderate grade. A large, flat rock on the left marks a slight break in the climb. Continue on up, cross a brook below a swamp, and continue to climb until after a final steep pitch you top out where the woods change from deciduous to big hemlocks. No, you are not nearly there yet! Stop for a snack and be glad you brought a large lunch and plenty to drink.

The trail runs down, level for a while, up and down and up, sometimes steeply, switching back and forth. The junction with Pisgah Mountain Trail provides a choice. The climb up to the summit is very steep, although the first part is quite moderate. People with lots of energy—particularly those who want something to do while other members of the party rest—can make a side trip.

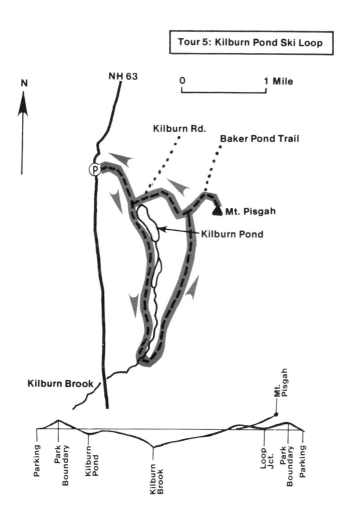

From the Pisgah Mountain junction, the trail continues up and down through various types of forest for about half a mile to a bridge and the junction with Kilburn Road. Turn left for 0.1 mile, mostly uphill, to the start of the Kilburn Loop. You have been here before. Turn right for the last three-quarters of a mile uphill and down again to your car.

Pisgah Mountain Trail

The Pisgah Mountain Trail runs downhill, climbs a ridge, and drops to a little marshy area, then climbs up to a small notch (0.4 mile) where the Baker Lake (foot) Trail turns left. The trail drops and then turns sharp right to slab up the northeast side of Pisgah Mountain, becoming increas-

Tree debris forms a pattern in the snow.

ingly steeper as it climbs. The summit is a small open spot with a limited view eastward. While some maps show this as the summit of Mt. Pisgah, others show the summit as being the next ridge over.

Additional Skiing

Many miles of park roads are available for skiing and are open to snowmobiles as well. More trails are being constructed, some from different access roads to the park.

6

ODIORNE POINT STATE PARK

Distance: 2-mile loop, can be repeated with variations
Difficulty: minimal
Surface: paved/trail

Maps: Odiorne Point State Park Map, USGS Kittery, Maine 7½′

The Piscataqua River is the boundary between New Hampshire and Maine. Below the I-95 and US-1/BYP1 bridges the river divides around an island. On the northeast point of the island is the U.S. Coast Guard station and Fort Constitution; on the southeast point is Fort Stark. Odiorne Point, the northernmost spot on the New Hampshire coast, lies south on the mainland.

On May 15, 1622, David Thomson received from the crown a 6,000 acre grant in New Hampshire. On April 16, 1623, he and his party landed at Pannaway, as the point was then called by the Indians, and started the first British settlement in the state. It grew as a farming and fishing settlement and later a summer colony.

The area at the present Coast Guard station was first fortified in 1632. In 1692, after more extensive work, it was named Fort William and Mary. Prior to his famous ride to Lexington, Paul Revere carried a message to the area that the British were coming to take over the fort, and the Sons of Liberty carted off some cannons and gunpowder.

After the Revolution it was renamed Fort Constitution and renovated in time for the War of 1812. During the Spanish-American War and World Wars I and II, Portsmouth Harbor was protected by mines laid from here.

The fortifications at Odiorne Point were built in 1942, to house two 16-inch naval guns, and were named Fort

Dearborn. The hills in the park camouflage the batteries
and other structures. After the war, most of the coastal
forts were scrapped and generally now are parks and
historical sites. The excellent Audubon Society of New
Hampshire Nature Center at Odiorne Point is not open in
the winter.

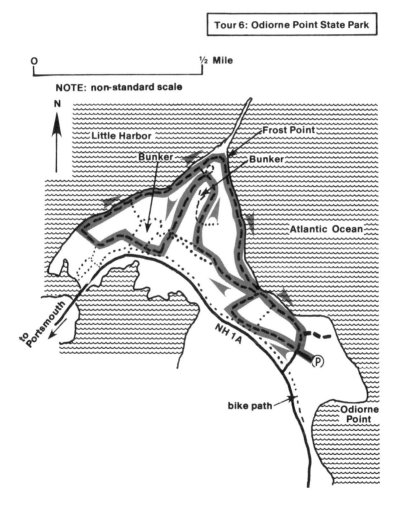

Tour 6: Odiorne Point State Park

Driving Directions

Odiorne Point State Park is on the coastal road NH-1A. It is 4 miles east of Portsmouth or 4.5 miles north of Rye Beach. The main parking area is plowed.

The Tour

From the parking lot, take the middle trail going west. Follow it, bearing right, then left, then right again to an old cement bunker. From the base, take a side trip up a trail climbing diagonally to the right up to the top of the bunker. Ski out to the north end for a panoramic view of the breakwater and harbor beyond. The trip back to the bottom the way you came is an easy slide.

Now continue on past the bunker out to the point and a good view across to the other side of Little Harbor. The large white building opposite is the late nineteenth-century resort hotel, Wentworth-by-the-Sea—now closed, but a reminder of the lifestyle of that era.

Continue on, past a second, and smaller, bunker and up to the boat launching area. From there bear right and follow the edge of the shore around Frost Point and back to the start.

This is just one of several possibilities at Odiorne Point. All the unplowed roads, walks, and trails are available for skiing. A bike path follows the southern boundary, roads cross the interior, and trails follow the shore. The area is too small to get lost in—make up your own choice of loops as long as your time lasts.

Because it is on the coast, the vegetation is different from most of the other ski trips in this book, and skiing along while watching waves rolling in and tankers passing by is a wonderful experience. While not available often because of slim snowfall, its very novelty leads to a friendliness and camaraderie notable even among skiers.

View of the ocean from Fort Dearborn.

WESTERN

7 CARDIGAN

	Back 80/Allieway/93Z	**Alexandria/Allieway**
Distance:	2.5-mile loop	3.5-mile loop
Difficulty:	moderate	moderate/difficult
Surface:	old road/trail	trail
Map:	AMC Cardigan	

Mt. Cardigan is better known for climbing than skiing, and trails tend to be challenging. On the east side of the mountain is a network of interconnected hiking and ski trails, becoming steeper and more difficult at higher elevations. Ski mountaineers will find the trails exhilarating; strong intermediates can find pleasure on the lower slopes; novices will find few options.

The route described is one of the easiest, and it gives a sample of what is available.

Parking and trail use is available to everyone. However, the Appalachian Mountain Club Lodge, located at the parking area, is not open to the public during the winter. For information on ski workshops and recreational ski weekends contact the AMC in Boston.

Driving Directions
From Bristol, take NH-3A north. At the south end of Newfound Lake, turn left at the blinking light onto West Shore Road. After 2 miles, go straight where West Shore Road turns right. Continuing past various side roads, and watching for AMC signs, bear right at the fork at 3.1 miles, left at the next fork at 6.3 miles, and right and shortly right again at 7.4 miles. The AMC lodge is reached at 8.9 miles.

This dirt road is steep and winding. After storms, the town usually plows and sands it well, but not necessarily immediately; it is not recommended for ordinary traffic when snow has occurred overnight or is forecast.

Back 80, Allieway and 93Z Trails

Continue up the road past the AMC lodge parking lot. The Back 80 Trail leaves to the right, before the open practice ski slope. It climbs steeply, following the brook; farther up the gradient decreases slightly. The trail forks just beyond the Short Circuit Ski Trail junction, with the Back 80 heading right and a ski trail going left. They are very similar, but the left-hand is recommended. In a quarter mile, the Allieway (spelled with an "i" on ski map and double "e" on sign) Ski Trail crosses, marked only by red tape on the trees. Turn right onto it. Here the going is narrow, but fairly level, and flanked by little spruce trees.

The Allieway Trail ends when it reaches the Back 80 Trail, which jogs right at the junction. Go straight ahead on the Back 80 Trail. Soon there is a cellar hole on the right, opposite where the Back 80 Trail turns uphill. The Back 80 Loop goes straight ahead. Take it. It drops steeply for a way and crosses the 93Z Trail. Turn right.

The 93Z is steep but fairly wide. It switches back at a brook, re-approaches it, and crosses it, gradually becoming less steep. Beyond the Short Circuit junction it comes onto an old road and climbs slightly. You can continue ahead on the 93Z trail until it ends at the road or turn right on the Manning Trail, about three-quarters of a mile after the Short Circuit junction. The Manning Trail leads through a beautiful grove of large trees before coming out in the field east of the lodge.

An easy trip would be to go up the end of this route on the 93Z trail as far as desired and return. The Manning Trail can be found by crossing the field to the right of the "Little House." Go to the right of the fireplace, bear right at station "B" on the nature trail, continue through the trees, and turn left on the 93Z. (Note that the Manning Trail crosses the road here and climbs Mt. Cardigan on its other direction.)

Alexandria, Allieway Ski Trails

For the Alexandria Ski Trail, continue up the road past the lodge and the practice hill and turn left at the sign. The trail drops down to a narrow bridge, then climbs at a moderate

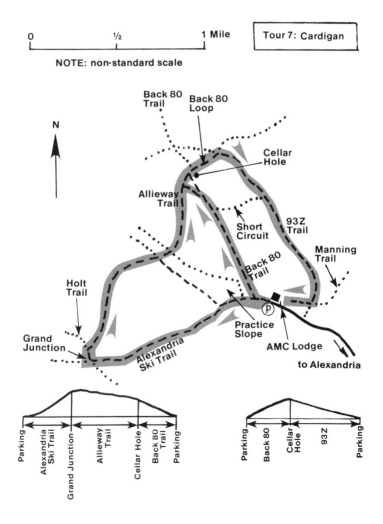

grade to a foot bridge. Keep right on the ski trail instead of crossing the bridge.

At the top of the hill, at Grand Junction, turn right on the Holt Trail, and immediately another right onto the Allieway, which crosses a brook and climbs in switchbacks up to a ridge, then circles and drops down along the other side. This trail is not especially well marked (only the hiking trails are blazed) but may be tracked out. In most places it is fairly obvious, especially where it runs through borders of little spruces. There are few signs at the junctions, but all trails to the right downhill lead back to the lodge. You can return down the Back 80. If you miss it and reach the cellar hole, go back to the last trail.

Ice crystals on a frozen pond.

FRANCONIA NOTCH

Franconia, Lincoln

Distance: 8.25 miles one way
Difficulty: mostly minimal
Surface: paved bike-path

Maps: DeLorme, Franconia Notch State Park Map, AMC Franconia

When Franconia Notch Parkway was built, much of the way was superimposed on an existing road. Non-automotive traffic was, and is, restricted, so a special path was built to accommodate cyclists. Since the Franconia Bike Path is not maintained after snowfall, it is available for winter recreation, although these days its future as a cross-country ski trail is up in the air. The snowmobile clubs, which have been barred from the Pemigewassett Wilderness, need a through north-south corridor, and the bike path is their most logical route. To compensate, the Pemi hiking trail has been cleared and reestablished as a parallel ski trail. If conditions are otherwise, follow the informational signs. The alternate ski trail, not being graded and paved, is somewhat more difficult than the bike path.

The bike path runs from the Flume parking lot to the end of I-93, three miles north of the Old Man of the Mountain. Throughout, there is little gradient so the trip can be done in either direction, or up and back from any of the parking lots in between. I chose a southbound route, which is the more favorable way to ski the whole bike path—there is slightly more downgrade, and the wind is usually behind you. The bike path gives access, much better than the interstate, to the scenic attractions of Franconia Notch. Going south, you pass views to Artist's Bluff overlooking Echo Lake, the Tramway, and the ski slopes on Cannon Mountain. There's an excellent view of the Old Man of the Mountain, and a short side trip leads to the Basin and the icy lacework in the Pemigewasset River.

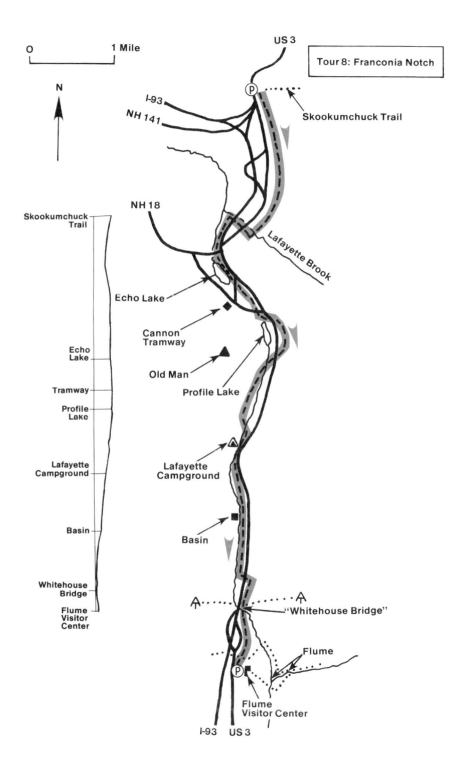

In addition, the paved surface allows skiing with less snow cover in the sheltered spots. Watch for windblown areas at the top of the Notch.

Driving Directions

From I-93 north of Woodstock, follow the signs to the Flume parking lot. The bike bath starts at the northwest corner, to the extreme left as you drive in. If you are doing a car shuttle, leave one vehicle here.

Continue driving north on I-93, which is called Franconia Notch Parkway in this area. Beyond the Old Man parking lot and the Cannon Tramway, bear right (eastbound, toward Twin Mountain) on US-3. Just as the one way traffic ends, Skookumchuck Trail parking lot is on the right.

Bike Path

The bike path starts at the sign at the south end of the Skookumchuck Trail parking lot. The road is wide and straight, with views ahead of Eagle Cliff and Cannon Mountain. From the high bridge over Lafayette Brook, look southeast toward Mt. Lafayette.

As it approaches the Notch, the bike path drops and crosses under the interstate. Be cautious here; the path may be bare and/or icy under the overpass, and skis might have to be removed. The path then climbs gradually to the head of the Notch at three miles and passes east of Echo Lake.

After crossing the access road to the Tramway, it passes east of Profile Lake and crosses back under the interstate to the east. As it comes close to the road at the bottom of a dip, look up to the right to the Old Man of the Mountain profile, high on the skyline of Cannon Cliff.

After a short downhill run, the path crosses back to the

west side of the interstate and runs fairly level to Lafayette Campground at five and a quarter miles. Through the parking lot, where the hiking trails turn right across a bridge, the bike path continues straight ahead. Beyond here the valley is wider, and the bike path farther from the road. The Pemi hiking trail crosses several times.

At the Basin, six and three quarter miles, several tourist trails follow the stream, which is attractive in its winter coat

Ski trail signs in Franconia Notch.

with ice trim. Return to the bike path partway down the long hill below, which is a good run. At the bottom the path crosses back under the interstate for the last time. The last mile to the Flume is mostly level with some upgrade, which at the end of the day seems steeper than it actually is.

Other Skiing

For a party with one car, the best and easiest part of the trip is the three miles from the Basin to the Profile Lake and return. But to park on the west side of the interstate at the Basin, if you are coming from the south, it's necessary to drive all the way to the Tramway to reverse direction.

Skiing to the Flume is also possible, following the summer trails. Most of the way is easy to moderate, but use care near the Flume and the covered bridge.

MINK BROOK TRAIL

Hanover

	Mink Brook Trail	**Harris/Mink Brook Trails**
Distance:	2.3 miles one way	2.6 miles one way
Difficulty:	easy	easy
Surface:	trail/logging road	trail/logging road

Map: USGS Mascoma 15'

The Mink Brook Trail on Moose Mountain is an easy and pleasant trip. Although well used by skiers, it doesn't have snowmobile or foot traffic and it holds the snow well. The gradient is usually gentle, with steep places at the brook crossings, but the brooks are unbridged and small. Overall, the Mink Brook Trail is well signed but generally unblazed. Skiers may opt for an easier and shorter one-way trip by using the Harris Trail for access. This starts with a moderate climb followed by a long level, and gentle downhill run.

Driving Directions

From Etna, a village east of Hanover, take King Road east for 2.3 miles. At a "T" intersection turn left on Ruddsboro Road. In 0.9 mile turn right on Dana Road. In 0.3 mile turn right again. A plowed parking lot is 0.2 mile on the left.

Mink Brook, Harris Trails

The Mink Brook Trail starts at the west end of the parking lot. It falls slightly downhill before crossing Mink Brook, then climbs steeply to the top of a bank, where an unmarked trail turns left. Bearing right, follow along the brook, crossing back to the right. The grade is mostly gentle here, with only a few steep spots. At two tenths of a mile, an expert trail leads right; keep left. At six tenths of a mile, bear right steeply uphill on a more obvious trail.(Be warned, this turn is easy to miss on the return!)

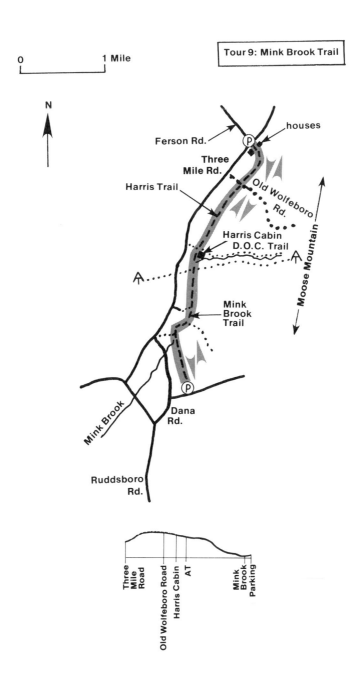

From the top of this grade, the remainder of the route is wider and more level for the next mile and a half, although there are still occasional dips.

At a little over a mile the Appalachian Trail, blazed in white, crosses. The Harris Trail, once the route of the Appalachian trail two relocations ago, is now your route. This is just one of five in this book that cross or follow the Appalachian Trail, which runs from Mount Katahdin in Maine to Springer Mountain in Georgia.

Continue ahead following the blue blazes. Shortly an expert ski trail leaves right, and at a mile and a quarter a DOC (Dartmouth Outing Club) trail leads to Harris Cabin, a private, locked cabin. Continue along on a nearly level old road. The old Wolfeboro Road crosses. All of these side trails climb steeply to the ridge of Moose Mountain and are not recommended.

At two and a quarter miles, the blazed trail bears left sharply and soon starts a steep downward run for a quarter mile to Three Mile Road. At this point, turn around and return to the start.

Harris Trail, Mink Brook Trail

Parties with two cars who wish a shorter trip can start at the northern end of the trail and ski south. This gives a short moderate climb at the start, followed by a long level to a downhill run. After a thaw it would be well to ski in from the south and check the condition of the Mink Brook crossing before committing to the trip. All problem crossings are in the first quarter mile.

After leaving a car at the end of the Mink Brook Trail, continue north on Three Mile Road for two and a half miles to Ferson Road. The trail (no sign) leaves 100 yards south of Ferson Road to the east.

A road climbs steeply through a field between two houses. Where the new road enters the woods, bear left slightly along the edge of the woods and pick up the narrow, blue-blazed trail, which parallels the road to the north. The trail climbs east at a moderate grade, and then bears round to the right along a shelf, picking up an old road and continuing south.

All of the major trail crossings are well marked except for one, also blue-blazed, which diverges to the right south of the Appalachian Trail. Keep left at that junction. Also watch for a left turn halfway down a steep hill where the Mink Brook Trail bears left off of the more prominent trail.

Sidestepping across an unfrozen brook.

Distance: 5.3 mile loop
Difficulty: easy/moderate
Surface: old logging road/trail

Maps: AMC Chocorua-Waterville, DeLorme

The Three Ponds ski trip described is a loop that goes up one valley, crosses a low height-of-land, and follows another stream back. The loop can be done in either direction (and I have) or in and out from either end. The distance between the trailheads is short, so the trip can be made without a second car.

Since brooks and swamps are crossed, the trip is best done following very cold weather when the water will be frozen. Breaking through the ice is not uncommon, but the brooks are small and the swamps usually not deep. Beaver workings are extensive and have altered the shape and size of the ponds.

Driving Directions

From Rumney, reached from NH-25 west of Plymouth, take the Stinson Lake Road north. At 5 miles from the Baker River bridge, pass through the town of Stinson Lake. Continue up the west side of the lake. At 6.7 miles the Three Ponds parking lot is on the left, partway down a steep hill. Usually it is not plowed, so you may wish to leave gear and excess people here. The driver can take the car another quarter mile to the bridge over Brown Brook, where there is a pull-off, and walk back.

Three Ponds Loop

Starting from the parking lot, follow Three Ponds Trail, bearing left on the loop. The trail here is narrow and climbs

0 _____ 1 Mile

Tour 10: Three Ponds Loop

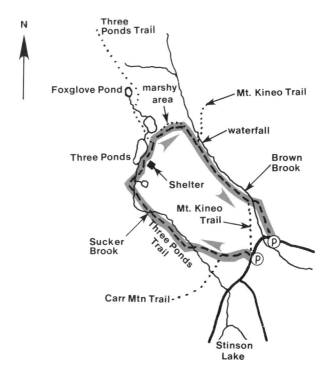

N

Three
Ponds Trail

Foxglove Pond   marshy
area

Mt. Kineo Trail

waterfall

Three Ponds

Brown
Brook

Shelter

Mt. Kineo
Trail

Sucker
Brook

Three Ponds
Trail

P

P

Carr Mtn Trail

Stinson
Lake

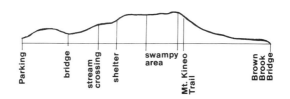

Parking — bridge — stream crossing — shelter — swampy area — Mt. Kineo Trail — Brown Brook Bridge

quite steeply for a short distance for one of the most difficult segments on the whole trip. It levels off, passes the
Carr Mountain Trail to the left, and at a mile drops down to
cross Sucker Brook on a log bridge. The proper way to
cross a foot bridge with a handrail is to put the appropriate
hand on the railing and grasp both ski poles with the other
hand. Move your skis carefully in the track. Avoid plunging
the pole into the snow on the bridge and weakening the
sides of the snow track.

The trail now picks up an old road and follows it up along
the brook, crossing back and forth three times. After a little
more than two miles, the trail passes a pond on the left. A
trail on the right leads up to a shelter on a rise overlooking
the pond, a scenic spot for lunch.

The Forest Service maintains many of these "Adirondack
shelters" in the White Mountain National Forest. They are
available on a first-come, first-served basis and often have
a pit toilet and a fireplace. The roof is cleverly designed to
drip water down the cook or fire tender's neck.

Return down the far side of the rise to the trail and continue a quarter mile to a trail junction. The area around this
spot is the scene of much current beaver working.
Chewed trees are in evidence all around; dams alter the
character of the ponds and flood water through the low
areas. The Three Ponds Trail continues north. For a side
trip, cross the beaver dam and follow it to the upper pond,
or farther if you wish—the height-of-land is another two-
and-a-half miles.

To complete your loop, turn right on the Donkey Hill Cut-off,
which is sparsely blazed in yellow paint. To add to the con-
fusion, some boundary lines in the area are blazed in the
same color yellow.

To tell the difference: Trail blazes are usually vertical rectangles, 2 inches by 4 to 6 inches (or occasionally round) placed on a tree so as to be visible in either direction from the last blaze. This means blazes on opposite sides of the tree, with the blazes facing each other, except on a curve when they are slightly offset. A double blaze, one above the other, indicates a sharp change of direction. Property blazes are large splotches painted along the outside of a tree parallel to the property line. Property lines usually do not have a footway.

Crossing a hiker footbridge.

The Donkey Hill Cut-off circles along beside a swamp, crosses a gully (where the property line blazes are off to the right), and contours wide and level across to the next marshy area. Where the trail climbs high to the right along the side hill the going is much easier next to the edge of the marsh, keeping the hill on the right. For much of the way, the blazes can be seen above.

Pass an open area where Mount Kineo stands out to the left. Circle right and left along the marsh, keeping adjacent to the high ground on the right. Where the marsh ends, and a small ridge comes in on the left and the trees get bigger, climb up over a small rise on the right on a bearing of 100° and rejoin the trail. Continue down the far side, swing a little more southward, and come out at the trail junction with the Mount Kineo Trail at the top of a waterfall. If you should be too far left and come out on a stream, turn right and follow it to the junction.

Turn right on the Mount Kineo Trail, following an old road on the near side of Brown Brook. The going is steep for a tenth of a mile past two waterfalls, but the gradient gradually lessens. Because the road is badly eroded, with streams crossing back and forth, some circling is necessary to find the best route.

Near the end, a new logging road approaches from the left. The trail forks, with both sides dropping steeply to the road at the bridge and your car.

11 TUNNEL BROOK

Benton, Glencliff

Distance: 3.2 miles one way
Difficulty: easy/moderate
Surface: hiking trail

Maps: AMC Franconia, DeLorme

A series of beaver ponds, lying deep in a notch between Mt. Clough and Mt. Moosilauke, is reached by the Tunnel Brook Trail, which runs from Benton to the North-South Road near Glencliff. The trail can be skied from either direction. The northern one is longer and easier, but the southern one is my favorite and is described below.

Although narrow in places, most of the trail is an easy grade. The small stream crossings are the most difficult part, and in heavy snow conditions finding the route in the area of the beaver ponds may require imagination.

Driving Directions

If you are coming up NH-25 from the south, the lower ridge of Mt. Moosilauke will stand out on the right. From this angle Mt. Clough, on the west, seems more narrow and pointed, with the deep notch visible between them.

From NH-25 in Glencliff Village (about 4 miles north of Warren), turn east toward Glencliff Sanatorium. In 1 mile, at the far end of the field, the North-South Road, marked by a Forest Service sign, turns left. Even if it is plowed, park on the Glencliff Road, as there is no parking at the trailhead.

Tunnel Brook Trail

The North-South Road descends to the bridge over Jeffers Brook and passes the Town Line Trail (a possible side trip of a mile) on the left. Tunnel Brook Trail takes the second

road to the right — a quarter mile from the Glencliff Road —
which ends at a private cabin. Continue on, following the yellow blazes, on the west side of the brook.
The first half mile is the hardest. The trail crosses Jeffers
Brook, continuing on the north side of Slide Brook, in one
place traversing a steep slope above the brook. It crosses
a northern tributary and Slide Brook, continuing on the

Traversing along a brook.

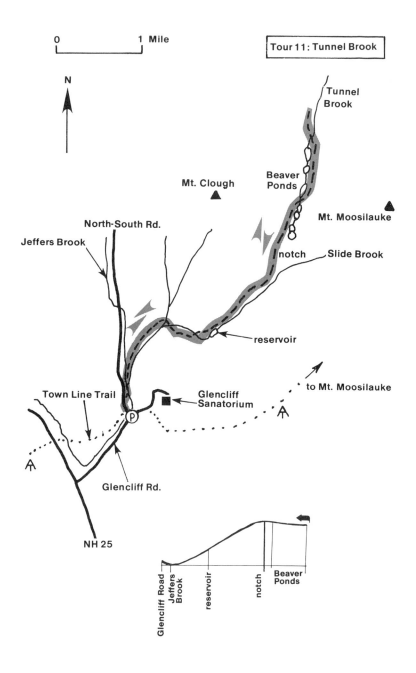

0 ___ 1 Mile

N

Tour 11: Tunnel Brook

Tunnel Brook

Mt. Clough

Beaver Ponds

Mt. Moosilauke

North-South Rd.

Jeffers Brook

notch   Slide Brook

reservoir

to Mt. Moosilauke

Town Line Trail

Glencliff Sanatorium

P

Glencliff Rd.

NH 25

Glencliff Road
Jeffers Brook
reservoir
notch
Beaver Ponds

south side. All crossings are steep and probably should be sidestepped. From the far side of the last crossing of Slide Brook, the trail climbs and reaches a small reservoir in just over a mile. The trail continues on the west side of the brook, mostly at a moderate grade, with one steeper section.

Near the head of the notch, the first pond can be seen on the right at two and a quarter miles. All of the famed beaver activity is on Tunnel Brook, which drains to the north. The ponds are hard to count—if a pond has a dam in the middle, is it one pond or two? How big a puddle is a pond?—but there are at least seven. The view of the notch is impressive, with the steep walls on both sides and the scars of massive slides.

The trail continues along the west side of the ponds, sometimes narrow among the overhanging evergreens. The summer trail may not be the best winter route. If you choose to ski on the ponds beware of soft spots, especially where little brooks enter and near dams.

After four or five ponds (three ponds from the north) the trail crosses through a brushy area to the east side. You can return from here or continue along the last two ponds before turning around. Beyond the last pond, the trail drops and soon crosses the brook to the west side.

·

CENTRAL

12 FLAT MOUNTAIN PONDS

Waterville, Sandwich

Distance: 5.9 miles each way
Difficulty: mostly easy/moderate
Surface: eroded logging railroad bed
Maps: AMC Chocorua-Waterville, DeLorme

The Flat Mountain Ponds are set in a bowl between the Flat Mountains on the north and south, the Sandwich Mountains on the west, and the Tripyramids and Sleepers on the east. The trip is less difficult than the distance would indicate as most of the way is fairly easy going, with only a couple of steep places. None of the stream crossings are bridged. It is a popular objective for both skiers and snowmobiles, but if you can manage to avoid the crowd, the trip can be a wild and rewarding experience.

Driving Directions

From the junction of NH-113 and 113A in North Sandwich, go north on 113A. In 1.7 miles you will pass the Whiteface Fire Station. Continue another 1.3 miles; NH-113A bears right, take the road to the left, and in 0.1 mile turn left on Bennett Street. After another 1.7 miles, shortly beyond an old farmhouse on the left, the road forks. The road to the left is not usually plowed, but a parking area at the junction is. Park here.

Flat Mountain Pond Trail

Ski down the unplowed road to the left, through the Swift River Tree farm. The going is almost level for a mile to Jose's Bridge (pronounced "Josie"), which is the trailhead in summer. Do not cross the bridge. Take the Flat Mountain Pond Trail straight ahead past the gate. Unobtrusive arrows on brown signs mark all dubious turns.

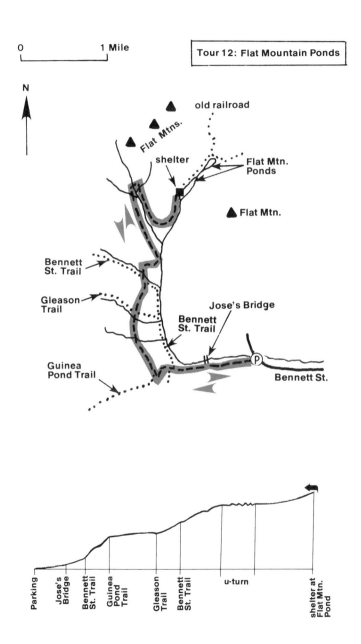

0   1 Mile

Tour 12: Flat Mountain Ponds

N

old railroad

Flat Mtns.

shelter

Flat Mtn.
Ponds

Flat Mtn.

Bennett
St. Trail

Gleason
Trail

Jose's Bridge

Bennett
St. Trail

Guinea
Pond Trail

P

Bennett St.

Parking

Jose's
Bridge

Bennett
St. Trail

Guinea
Pond
Trail

Gleason
Trail

Bennett
St. Trail

u-turn

shelter at
Flat Mtn.
Pond

The road climbs gently along the brook for a half mile to the Bennett Street Trail. (This trail follows the brook to the right, then climbs steeply to the summit of Sandwich Mountain, crossing our trail later.) Continue ahead, keeping right at a nearly imperceptible fork. This is the start of the steepest climb on the trip for a tenth of a mile, then a levelish slab to the left, and another steep climb to the old logging railroad grade. The hill is steep enough to require herringboning or sidestepping for some of the climb. The packed snowmobile trail forms a slippery trough even with a light coating of fresh snow. Instead of working in the concave trough, move out onto the convex edge, which will give a much more comfortable angle to herringbone. Likewise with the sidestep, instead of trying to fit the skis into a "U," have them straight with only the tips in the trail and the heels out on the side. The skis can also point slightly downhill for greater comfort without the chance of losing control.

At the junction, the Guinea Pond Trail follows the grade west to Guinea Pond and ultimately the Sandwich Notch Road. The Flat Mountain Pond Trail turns right. Note this spot for the return. As expected, the railroad grade climbs gently. Over the years it has washed out some, and all the culverts and trestles are missing. Many minor dips break the even gradient.

Even though unbridged, the streams are tiny and the crossings should present no problem. The route is on the east side of the Sandwich range, in the shadow in the afternoon, a good reason to start home early, and holds snow and ice well. Just under a mile, after the first of three big ravines, the yellow-blazed Gleason Trail crosses.

At this elevation the route is lined with good-sized birch trees. After a fresh snowfall, their white is less impressive than against the bright green of spring, or contrasted with the dark reds and yellows of fall. The Bennett Street Trail crosses in half a mile, just before the next large ravine. A few remaining timbers from the trestle can be seen strewn down the bank. They were removed partly because they were getting old, but also to prevent vehicles from driving to the pond. The third big ravine may be the steepest.

Up to this point, the trail/railroad follows the contour along a major stream. Now it circles the headwaters, making a hairpin turn to follow back along the other side of the valley, the sharpest turn on any logging railroad in the area. At the apex of the turn three brooks are crossed—one three times —as well as some wet areas. Usually the snow bridges are

Flat Mountain Pond.

adequate, but the approaches are steep, and sidestepping may give greater control in an area where a fall might result in breaking through into the water. Note any particular problems for the return, and remember where they are.

After crossing this level, open area, the last mile of the trail circles back on the other side of the stream, contouring around the point of land and following the outlet brook from Flat Mountain Pond. Now in evergreens, it climbs more steeply before leveling off beside the stream. Here, the wider outlet to the lake comes into sight on the right. The shelter is on the far side of the hummock ahead; watch for the trail junction and take the trail to the right, which leads to the dam. The shelter is on the right with a view down the lake.

Because the shelter and the pond are exposed to the wind, you may wish to dress warmly for your rest stop. The mountain that stands out at the end of the lake is South Tripyramid. Following the west side of the pond, the Sleeper Ridge toward Mt. Whiteface comes into view. All the near surrounding mountains, both northeast and southwest, are called "Flat Mountain."

A second pond lies to the northeast. The trail along the west side of the first pond is very difficult even by foot in summer; if the ice is solid, follow the shore and either rejoin the trail at the northwest end of the first pond or cut through the woods to the upper pond. From here, a railroad spur heads north for a short distance into a swampy area. Do not walk on the ice near the mouth of the brook, as it may be soft. Follow the railroad grade on the shore.

For about three-quarters of the return, skis run easily with only occasional striding or double poling needed to keep moving. Except for the dips there is no true uphill, but because of them, the return is slower than it might otherwise be.

13 GREELEY PONDS

Lincoln, Livermore

Distance: 2.2 miles one way
Difficulty: moderate/difficult
Surface: ski trail

Maps: USFS Pemigewasset, DeLorme

The Greeley Ponds lie between the steep cliffs of Mt. Osceola and Mt. Kancamagus, and are reached by a trail running from the Kancamagus Highway south over Mad River Notch to Waterville Valley. The upper pond at one time was a favorite camping spot, with a shelter on the sandy shore. But it was too well used and abused, and in 1964 the ponds were designated a "Scenic Area." The shelter was removed, and fires and camping restricted. In 1986 the Mt. Osceola Trail was relocated from the shore of the pond to the top of the notch.

Driving Directions

The Greeley Pond Ski Trail is at the western end of the Kancamagus Highway, at the south side of a southeast hairpin turn. It is 4.3 miles east of the Wilderness Trail, 4.4 miles west of Kancamagus Pass, 1.2 miles west of the big hairpin turn, and 0.3 mile west of the Greeley Pond Hiking Trail. The only marking is a ski touring sign. Park beside the road.

Greeley Ponds Ski Trail

Many old roads lead to Greeley Ponds. Of these, the hiking trail is the easternmost, and the ski trail is the westernmost. A brook runs up the valley between them.

The ski trail, which is marked by blue triangles, starts to the left of the ski-touring sign, up a little gulch. Bear right at the fork, within sight of the road. The trail avoids all brooks, but in places it is steep.

At the height-of-land, the well-worn trail to Mt. Osceola is crossed. Its junction with the hiking trail is within sight to the left. The ski trail continues ahead, joins the hiking trail, and passes a large boulder. It diverges right again to avoid two log bridges, rejoining the hiking trail near the shore of the upper pond, which it follows down the west bank.

The site of the old shelter is on the far side of the pond, at a clearing on the southeast end. The large boulders fallen from the cliff above make it worth visiting. Use care in crossing over to it; the summer trail crosses the outlet brook, which may be tricky. If you cross the pond, stay well away from the outlet, where the ice may be soft.

Herringboning.

Continuing south, the ski trail diverges first left, then right, then left again before rejoining the hiking trail. Follow the line of least resistance downhill to the lower pond, where the ski trail follows along the western shore until it crosses to the east side and down to Waterville Valley.

The best view up to Mad River Notch is from a knoll at the southwest end of this pond.

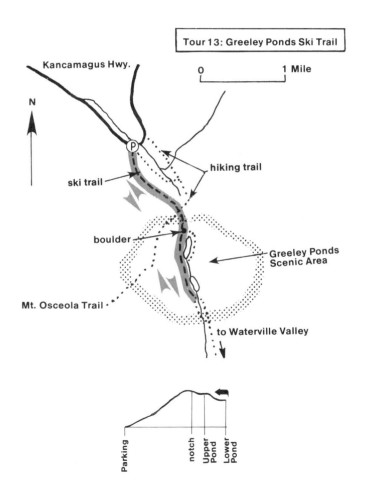

UPPER NANAMOCOMUCK SKI TRAIL

Livermore, Albany

	Whole Trail	Church Pond Loop	To Church Pond Loop from east
Distance:	9.3 miles	2.2 miles (add 1.7 to through trip)	4 miles each way
Difficulty:	moderate/difficult	minimal/moderate	easy/moderate
Surface:	ski trail	hiking trail	ski trail

Map: USFS Conway

Nanamocomuck was the son of Passaconaway, the brother of Wonalancet, and the father of Kancamagus. Tourists are big on Indian names. The trail that is named for him is maintained by the U.S. Forest Service. It parallels the Kancamagus Highway on the far side of the Swift River, which limits access and adds a great degree of remoteness. It is a long trip, and the upper part is steep. An easier version can be done by making a return trip from the east.

Driving Directions

The Kancamagus Highway runs from Lincoln to Conway, numbered NH-112. Take the Bear Notch Road to the north 11.8 miles west of Conway. Drive a mile up to the end of the plowed public road where the trail crosses. Start the easier trip here, or for the longer trip, leave one car here and return to the Kancamagus Highway and drive 7 more miles west to Lily Pond. The trail is at the east end of the pond — park at the wider place just beyond the trail.

Upper Nanamocomuck Ski Trail

As a one-way trip from Lily Pond to Bear Notch Road, this makes for a long day. Skiers should be confident of their stamina, as there is no convenient escape route. The ski trail crosses and follows several hiking trails in this section. Most of them can be skied, but the stream crossings are not bridged, and there is no longer a bridge on the Church Pond Road. The Swift River is not usually well frozen, and the crossings can be dangerous. Summer hikers usually wade across or go elsewhere when the water is high. Keep in mind that major signs for both hiking and ski trails are yellow on brown. Ski trails are marked with blue plastic diamonds and hiking trails with yellow paint. In particular, a yellow arrow often shows the direction in which the hiking trail leaves the ski trail: usually you will go the other way!

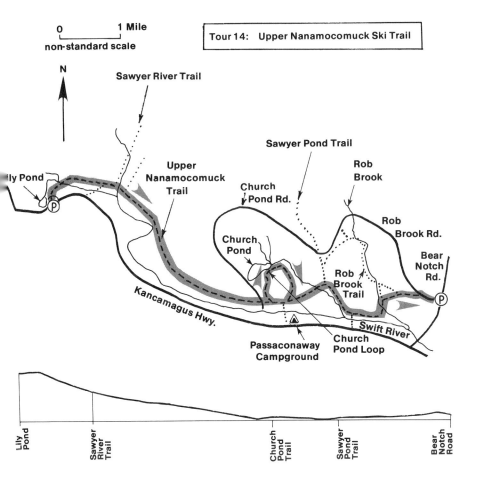

The first mile and a half from Lily Pond has steep down-grades, which may be moderate in good snow conditions and very difficult in poor. All streams are bridged with Forest Service ski bridges. Looking at ice formations in the rivers is one of the features of this trip.

The trail approaches the Swift River shortly above the junction with the Sawyer River Trail. The two trails coincide for a tenth of a mile, and then the Sawyer River Trail continues ahead and the Nanamocomuck Trail heads right, downhill, on a snowmobile trail. Just across the next bridge the snowmobile trail diverges left.

From here on, the downhills become easier. The trail circles around on a contour, up and down, high above the Swift River. Although it started in evergreens near Lily Pond, it now passes through small, open deciduous forest. Finally the trail enters an old logging road and follows it generally downhill to the Church Pond Road, which it crosses.

This marks the end of the long downhill section. In a quarter mile the west side of the Church Pond Loop Trail is reached. These junctions are marked both by brown wooden signs and notes on the blue diamonds. At this point the ski trail coincides with the hiking trail. At the end of the loop junction, bear left, and right again from the eastern end. This whole section from the Church Pond Road to the bridge over the Church Pond Outlet runs nearly level. Then it climbs to the junction with the Sawyer Pond Trail, turns right on it a short distance, then leaves left and follows the river bank. Finally it turns sharply left onto an arrow-straight old railroad bed, which it follows gradually uphill to another junction. (The railroad bed continues ahead a mile and a half to the Rob Brook Road, but the difficulty is increased by five unbridged crossings of Rob Brook.) This is part of the Bartlett and Albany Railroad, the only logging railroad that crossed a major height-of-land and went down the other side, requiring the engine to pull a load of logs uphill on the return.

The Upper Nanamocomuck Trail turns right onto an old logging road and climbs moderately around a hairpin turn to a swampy area, where it turns right onto the Rob Brook Trail at an unmarked "Y" junction. (In the reverse direction, turn left here.) The trail climbs moderately to the Rob Brook Road. Turn right for the last half mile up and downhill to the Bear Notch Road and your car. At the end of a long day, this seems a lot higher than it actually is.

Church Pond Loop

The side trip to Church Pond is very scenic, but adds over a mile and a half to the trip and may require breaking trail and finding the route for the entire distance. Coming down the Upper Nanamocomuck Trail, shortly after crossing Church Pond Road, bear sharply back left at the junction with the Church Pond Loop, blazed in yellow paint. The trail leads across an open area where the surrounding mountains stand out distinctly. In about a mile the trail climbs slightly onto a point overlooking Church Pond, with mountains as a backdrop. Continuing on, it follows the outlet brook a ways, goes up and down over a few minor lumps before leveling out the rest of the way back to the ski trail. Bear left on the Nanamocomuck Trail half a mile from where you left it.

Church Pond from the East

Start at Bear Notch Road. Follow the Upper Nanamocomuck Trail down the Rob Brook Road for half a mile to where it diverges left on the Rob Brook Trail. Turn left at the "Y" and then left again onto the railroad bed. The Church Pond Loop is reached a quarter mile beyond the bridge over the outlet and four miles from Bear Notch Road.

The loop is slightly more skiable in the clockwise direction. If it is not broken out, and/or you wish to shorten it, go in and out from this junction by taking a right. Otherwise continue on the ski trail for another half mile, bearing right at the loop junction and then bearing right again on the Church Pond Loop from the ski trail. Follow directions for Church Pond Loop. This total trip is 10 + miles, and remember it will be uphill returning.

An open area gives a good view of the surrounding mountains.

15 SANDWICH NOTCH

Distance: 5.5 miles one way
Difficulty: moderate
Surface: graded road

Maps: AMC Chocorua-Waterville, DeLorme

In 1803 the Sandwich Notch Road was improved to provide a better route from southeastern New Hampshire to the pioneers on the Pemigewasset River at Campton. At one time a busy settlement flourished up in those parts, and a logging railroad ran up the Beebe River from 1917-1942. Like many other places in New England, the area's labor-intensive farming faded away because of competition with the more capital-intensive farms in the Midwest.

Today modern highways follow the river valleys, crossing and recrossing the main river, and various large tributaries, on high bridges. Back in the old days, large streams were a problem. Even where the technology existed, bridges were expensive. Low bridges often washed away in spring floods, or were impassable in high water because the approaches were under water. Ferries were the usual solution, but they were only expedient where the traffic was sufficient to support their upkeep and they were unusable for half the year.

Roads through the low notches were usable except in blizzards and mud season. The spring mud season is caused by the frost melting in the upper part of the ground while the ground remains frozen lower down, so the water cannot drain away. Road work was done in lieu of taxes by local farmers. A little dig and fill with a pick and shovel would carve a track for a wagon out of the side of the hill. A few trees would span a small creek, with boards laid for tread. Footings could be made from rocks moved by crowbars and horses.

Much of the land in Sandwich Notch is now part of the White Mountain National Forest, and the present wild character of the area is being preserved. The road is maintained by the town of Sandwich and is "open" all year round, to appropriate use. Since heavy through traffic is discouraged, maintenance is minimal, and it is usable by ordinary vehicles only during the summer and early fall.

Driving Directions

From Center Sandwich at junction NH-109/113, take the unnumbered road northwest. There is a sign to Mead Base and Sandwich Notch. Bear left at the first fork, then keep straight ahead on the main road as other roads come in at angles. At 2.6 miles from Center Sandwich, the Sandwich Notch Road, unplowed, goes ahead while the plowed road to a farm and Mead Base turns right. There is a small plowed parking area.

Sandwich Notch Road

The Sandwich Notch Road climbs slightly at first, crosses a brook, then climbs more steeply. Halfway up, a parking area on the right marks the trail to Beebe Falls, on the upper reaches of the Bearcamp River. All trails from the parking area lead over to the brook; bear left upstream for the falls. Here a sheet of water dripping over an overhanging ledge forms a grotto with an ice front wall. Nearby, on the far side of the river in a small gulch under another small overhanging rock, is the fabled "cow cave," where, according to local legend, a farmer's cow spent the winter, emerging alive and kicking the following spring.

From the top of the hill, the road levels off, and then climbs again, past the Crawford-Ridgepole Trail on the left, half a mile from the falls. The road then runs among towering rocks, where church services were once held, and crosses three bridges. Wandering on past some old farm clearings, it drops down to the bridge over Beebe River three miles from the start. No sign exists of the former activity.

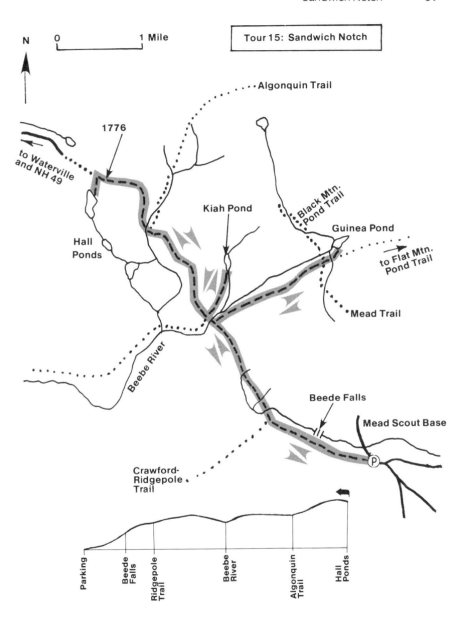

N

0   1 Mile

Tour 15: Sandwich Notch

Algonquin Trail

1776

to Waterville
and NH 49

Kiah Pond

Black Mtn.
Pond Trail

Guinea Pond

Hall
Ponds

to Flat Mtn.
Pond Trail

Mead Trail

Beebe River

Beede Falls

Mead Scout Base

P

Crawford-
Ridgepole
Trail

Parking

Beede
Falls

Ridgepole
Trail

Beebe
River

Algonquin
Trail

Hall
Ponds

Here you have at least three choices:

The first is to continue ahead on the road another two and a half miles to the height-of-land. Climb up a steep hill and continue up and down past the Algonquin Trail, on up to a small sign on a tree, "1776," giving the high point on the road. While this would be a reasonable objective, it is only another quarter mile more to Hall Ponds. After a brief downhill run you'll come to a good road on the left, leading fairly steeply downhill to the ponds.

Snowshoe rabbit tracks.

Kiah Pond

The second possibility is to cross the Beebe River bridge and take the road to the right. It runs slightly uphill for nearly a mile to Kiah Pond, where it ends.

Guinea Pond

Finally, you can take the road to the right on the south side of the Beebe River bridge. The old Beebe River Logging Railroad came up the Beebe River from Campton on the other side of the brook and continued on to Guinea Pond and Flat Mountain Ponds.

Continuing up the railroad grade, at a little more than a mile and a half, the Mead Trail is on the right, and the Black Mountain Pond Trail on the left. At one and three-quarters of a mile a side trail leads left to Guinea Pond. At four miles is the junction with Flat Mountain Pond Trail, and the railroad grade continues on.

16 SAWYER RIVER ROAD

	Sawyer River Road	Sawyer Pond Trail	Carrigain Notch
Distance:	4 miles	1.5 miles	4 miles
	(8 miles round trip)	(11 miles round trip)	(12 miles round trip)
Difficulty:	minimal/easy	moderate	difficult
Surface:	road	trail	trail

Maps: AMC Franconia, DeLorme

The Sawyer River Road, FR-49, is a gravel road that follows Sawyer River. During the summer it is open to the public for four miles; during the winter it is gated. Most of the grade is very gentle, only the hill at the beginning is steep.

The area was once the site of the Sawyer River Railroad, which operated for nearly 50 years. At that time the owners —the Saunders family—were virtually the only operation of their day to do selective timber cutting. In 1920 the state's taxation policy no longer favored conservation, and the remaining virgin timber was clear-cut. This, and the flood of 1927, which wiped out much of the railroad bed and bridges, caused the end of their operation and they sold the land to the Forest Service in 1936.

Driving Directions
The Sawyer River Road runs southwest from US-302, around a curve just north of the bridge over the Sawyer River, 4 miles west of Bartlett and 10 miles south of Crawford Notch. A small parking area is plowed on the side of the road. Use care pulling in and out, as it is on a curve.

Sawyer River Road
The road climbs steeply for just the first quarter mile. It follows high above the Sawyer River, passing Signal Ridge Trail on the right before the bridge over Whiteface Brook. After another mile the Carrigain Brook Road leaves right.

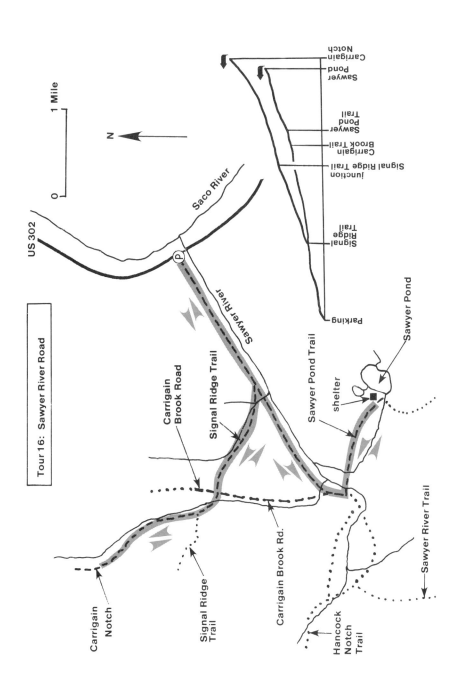

Tour 16: Sawyer River Road

US 302

Saco River

1 Mile

N

Carrigain Notch
Sawyer Pond

Sawyer Pond Trail
Carrigain Brook Trail
Signal Ridge Trail junction

Signal Ridge Trail

Parking

Sawyer River

Carrigain Brook Road
Signal Ridge Trail

Sawyer Pond Trail

Sawyer Pond

shelter

Carrigain Notch

Signal Ridge Trail

Carrigain Brook Rd.

Sawyer River Trail

Hancock Notch Trail

At four miles the road is gated. At times there is heavy foot traffic, especially along the first two miles.

Sawyer Pond

Sawyer Pond is one of the usual objectives on this trip, but the trail is considerably harder than the trip on the road. Approximately a quarter mile beyond the junction with the Carrigain Brook Road is a bridge to the left; cross it. The trail from the bridge is narrow and climbs steeply for a short distance, crosses a brook, and comes up on an old logging road. The going is better here but still not easy. The route crosses some small brooks as it circles a ridge, then drops down to the pond where a shelter is located. No trail exists around the pond.

Spruce trees after a fresh snowfall.

Carrigain Notch

This route follows Signal Ridge Trail and Carrigain Notch Trail. Since climbers use this trail frequently, and the stream crossings are difficult, try it only under very good conditions.

Turn right on Signal Ridge Trail from the Sawyer River Road two miles from the start, just before the bridge over Whiteface Brook. The most difficult brook crossing is a fifth of a mile in. (Hikers frequently bushwhack up the right bank of the brook, but this is less feasible for skiers.) The trail follows along the brook, where it may be icy in places, and is often steep. The Carrigain Brook Road crosses at nearly one and a half miles, where the trail crosses a low ridge to the next brook. Turn right on Carrigain Notch Trail at one and three-quarter miles.

The trail crosses Carrigain Brook, which it follows up to the notch. The lower part of the grade is on an old logging road, and not particularly steep, but a number of minor brooks and one extensive wet section a mile in may give problems.

Nearer the notch, the trail climbs away from the brook. Skiers sometimes follow the brook, making their own route.

Carrigain Brook Road

This road leaves from the north side of Sawyer River Road about three miles from the parking area. This road makes a possible loop with the Signal Ridge Trail. However, if you should desire to try this loop, go in on the Signal Ridge Trail, as there is a difficult crossing of the brook one-fifth mile from the road at the start. The Carrigain Brook Road crosses the Signal Ridge Trail at one and a half miles. One can go an indeterminate distance right on this road or turn left for a mile and a half back to the Sawyer River Road.

Waterville

Pine Flat/Yellow Jacket/Tritown Loop

Distance: 3.3-mile loop
Difficulty: difficult
Surface: ski trail/logging road

Map: USFS Ammonoosuc

In 1979, the Young Adult Conservation Corps of the U.S. Forest Service reconstructed some old roadways near the road to Waterville Valley for use as ski-touring trails. None of these trails is patrolled or groomed, and no fee is charged. As many of these trails are former logging roads, there are frequent signs of timber harvest.

It's possible to make several different loop trips from the Smarts Brook parking lot. The trip described below is about three miles long and should be considered Most Difficult. A parallel trip of intermediate difficulty will also be mentioned. If you are planning your own trips on this network, be aware that some of the trails are officially one way, and the Forest Service maps, signs, and descriptions are not necessarily consistent with each other.

Driving Directions

At Exit 28 off I-93, a tourist information center distributes literature that may be of interest to skiers. Follow Route 49 toward Waterville Valley, passing a traffic light at the intersection with Route 175 in Campton. At 4.2 miles from Campton, there is a small plowed parking lot on the right just across the Smarts Brook Culvert, which is the trailhead for the Smarts Brook (hiking) Trail. Park here.

Pine Flat/Yellow Jacket/Tritown Trails Loop

From the parking area, follow the Pine Flat Trail north along the highway at a level gradient. Take the right at a "Y" intersection (left is the easier bypass), which shortly reaches the mouth of the Smarts Brook Gorge with its overhanging boulders. The trail climbs directly up a steep slope. It's not as long as it feels, but if this gives you any trouble, turn back now or take the trail at the top that leads left to the bypass.

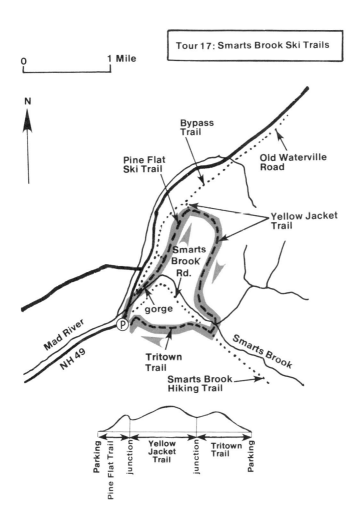

The Pine Flat Trail, which is one way uphill at this point, continues up the gorge. Much of the gorge is very scenic. Sheer rock walls rise upwards as much as 30 feet with multicolored icicles hanging from them. Unfortunately, you may find it difficult to enjoy, as much of the trail in this section slabs uphill on a narrow shelf where sidestepping is difficult: skins or good climbing wax are recommended. At the head of the gorge, the trail leaves the brook and attacks the side of the valley, climbing steeply over a ridge. There is a little easy going, and then the trail descends the other side at a moderate grade. Be sure to ski well under control here, as there is an exciting spot at the end, where the trail takes a sharp left turn and drops abruptly into a gully and equally abruptly up the other side.

Turn right on the woods road, which is the Yellow Jacket Trail, named for a variety of insect encountered during its construction but probably not while skiing it. The Yellow Jacket Trail, if followed left, leads to a junction where the bypass trail leads left back to the parking lot and the Old Waterville Road leads right to another parking area two and a half miles farther up Route 49. Although once the main highway, the Old Waterville Road has two steep sections that require intermediate ability. The Yellow Jacket Trail (right) follows a road at an easy to moderate uphill grade for more than a mile with a few dips. A small clearing is passed about midway. The trail approaches Smarts Brook again and then turns sharp right to cross it on a bridge. The yellow blazes that continue ahead at this turn mark the Smarts Brook hiking trail: it is not skiable at this point. Across the bridge, the Yellow Jacket Trail shortly ends at the Smarts Brook (logging) Road. This road can be skied left for some distance before it rejoins the hiking trail. To the right is an intermediate run downhill to the parking area.

For a more challenging return, follow the road right 200 yards and then turn left on the Tritown Trail. This trail passes

Watch out for thawing brooks.

through portions of the towns of Waterville Valley, Sandwich, and Thornton, but you are unlikely to see any of the boundary markings in the winter. It crosses a clearing and then ascends steeply to the ridge top, and then more moderately down the far side. Take the right fork at a clearing. The trail begins to level off and circles back to the Smarts Brook Road. This trail is poorly marked, and unless it is broken out, it should be attempted only by advanced skiers who are also good at route finding.

Whether you take the Tritown Trail or opt to return by the road, the last part of the road is one-way downhill. Continue on until you see the gate at the end of the road, then the trail suddenly leaves the road uphill, circles through the woods, and switchbacks to the road below the gate. This convolution is apparently to keep people from skiing into the gate. The trail then follows the shoulder of Route 49 back to the parking lot.

	East Branch	**Wilderness**
Distance:	5.5 miles one way	5.5 miles one way (total loop 11 miles)
Difficulty:	minimal/easy	minimal
Surface:	road/wide trail	logging railroad

Maps: AMC Franconia, DeLorme

The two trails that follow the East Branch of the Pemige-wassett River north from the Kancamagus Highway—the East Branch Trail on the east and the Wilderness Trail on the west—make the easiest long trip in this book, and perhaps in New Hampshire. They follow old logging rail-roads, Forest Service roads, and wide trails at water level grades. All or part of either trail can also be done as a return trip.

The trip will be described as a counterclockwise loop, which we found to be the easiest and most scenic.

Driving Directions

The Wilderness Trail parking area is a large lot, with outhouses, on the north side of the Kancamagus Highway, just east of the bridge over the East Branch. It is 5.3 miles east of I-93 at exit 32, and 8 miles west of Kancamagus Pass.

The information center at the exit 32 off-ramp has an excellent relief map of the White Mountains, as well as written and verbal information.

The major drawback to this trip is the frequency of car break-ins at the parking lot. Take the profit out of crime. DO NOT LEAVE ANYTHING OF VALUE IN YOUR CAR. Some people open the glove compartment and spread the maps out on the dash to show it doesn't contain wallets.

East Branch Trail

A large signboard by the river contains not only maps and current regulations, but some interesting history as well.

From this point, continue north on a Forest Service road for the first three miles. Short trails frequently lead left to the bank of the river. The first logging road right climbs up to a clearing high enough to see some of the nearer mountains.

A mile from the start, the road climbs slightly and circles on a higher level, within shouting distance of the trail. The trail to the left is more level, but bumpy, and crosses a small brook. The road gives a good, short downhill run to a wide bridge over the brook at the bottom. The East Branch is often in sight on the left; one good viewpoint high on a bluff looks both ways on the river.

The road ends at a point opposite the bridge over Franconia Brook, which can be seen from the shore. People often cross the river on the ice at this point, but neither the Forest Service nor I recommend it; the water is deep (and cold) and the current strong, and a collapse of the ice would have serious consequences.

A wide trail continues upstream, bearing more easterly. The views of the river are more frequent and more intimate, and the terrain is more interesting and only slightly more difficult than on the Wilderness Trail side. The trail runs close to the bank for a while, eventually veering higher up on the slope. Several small trickles of water are crossed, and finally the trail climbs steeply for a tenth of a mile to the unmarked but unmistakable Cedar Brook Trail. Turn left on an old logging road. (This turn could be unnoticeable going in the other direction after a fresh snow). The suspension bridge half a mile upstream can be seen from here.

Both the run down to, and crossing of, the bridge are easier than they look. This is your halfway point.

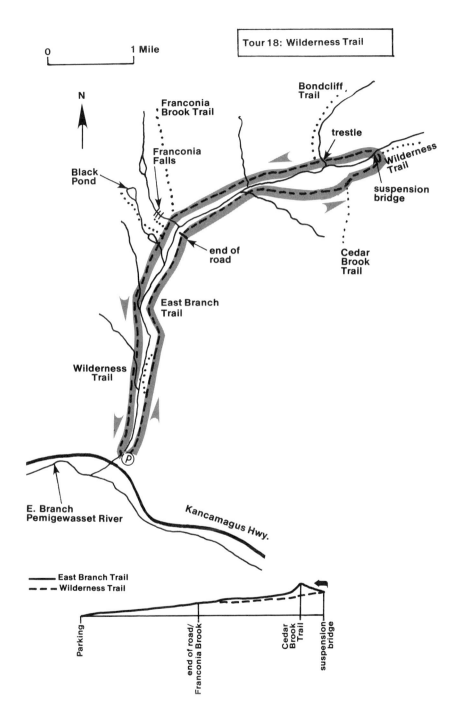

Tour 18: Wilderness Trail

0   1 Mile

N

Bondcliff Trail

Franconia Brook Trail

trestle

Wilderness Trail

Franconia Falls

suspension bridge

Black Pond

end of road

Cedar Brook Trail

East Branch Trail

Wilderness Trail

P

E. Branch Pemigewasset River

Kancamagus Hwy.

—— East Branch Trail
– – – Wilderness Trail

Parking

end of road/Franconia Brook

Cedar Brook Trail

suspension bridge

Wilderness Trail

Turn left on the far side of the bridge. The route follows an old railroad grade all the way back, which is straight and almost level for its whole length. This side is more heavily traveled.

In less than a mile the grade crosses the last remaining railroad trestle, which may not be around too much longer. From the Bondcliff Trail and the old Camp 16 campsite, the grade continues ahead, at times almost as far as the eye can see, broken only by an occasional eroded dip.

The Franconia Brook Trail diverges right at the top of the bank of Franconia Brook. The footbridge is at a lower level than the old trestle. People who don't like bridges usually don't like this one either, but I have never heard of anyone falling off! Some people ski, and some people walk, depending on the condition of the snow. Skiing is better unless it is very icy.

Now only two and three-quarter miles remain. Take a break, and let the red squirrels, chickadees, and blue jays relieve you of the rest of your lunch. A side trip up the west side of Franconia Brook to the falls will add a half mile to your trip.

The last part of the Wilderness Trail is heavily used by foot traffic and snowshoes, as well as skiers, and can be a cement sidewalk or a real mess depending on conditions. A quarter mile beyond the Franconia Brook trail, Black Pond Trail, an interesting but more difficult side trip, leads right.

The trail comes close to the river once, then bears farther away and passes the Osseo Trail a mile and a half from the end. For the last half mile the trail is closer to the river again at the top of a high bank. Around a curve to the right the suspension bridge is reached, leading left to the parking lot.

In case you did not heed the earlier warning, the Lincoln Police Station is on the left, four and a half miles west, in the same building as the fire station (0.9 miles east of I-93).

Additional Skiing

The East Branch and Lincoln Railroad was one of the longest lasting, best built, and latest operating of the logging railroads. The network of track ran for fifty miles, and it and its associated tote roads form the basis of most of the valley trails in the Pemigewasset Wilderness. Many of these trails are suitable for skiing. The only problem is that it crossed the rivers often, and the trestles are now missing.

Logging railroad trestle.

NORTHERN

Bethlehem

	Beaver Loop	Badger Loop	Moose Watch
Distance:	1.4-mile loop	2.3-mile loop	5.3-mile loop
Difficulty:	easy	moderate	moderate
Surface:	logging road	trail	trail

Map: USFS Ammonoosuc

The Beaver Brook Ski Trails are maintained by the U.S. Forest Service as part of the multi-use program for the White Mountain National Forest. A picnic area is provided with outhouses, tables, and grills available in winter. Three ski trails offer varying length and difficulty. All trails are one-way loops, coinciding at the start; all are marked with the same blue plastic diamonds.

Driving Directions

The Beaver Brook Rest Area is on the south side of US-3, located 8 miles east of Franconia Notch and 4 miles west of Twin Mountain. All trails start at an information sign midway on the small loop road.

Beaver Loop

Leave the parking area just left of the information sign. Go through a patch of woods to the edge of a clearing and the loop junction where the Badger and Moose Watch trails return.

Take the right, pass the return loop of Beaver Trail on the left. Cross a brook on a bridge (all major brooks are bridged) and climb the gentle rise on a wide logging road, with views of the surrounding mountains through the trees. Much recent logging is evident, and skid roads are frequently crossed. The ski trail takes a sharp left where the road goes ahead. Cross a level area and make a short, steep climb to a junction where the Badger Trail takes a sharp right.

The Beaver Trail follows a wide road, crosses a bridge, and climbs a little more. A "caution" sign marks a short, steep spot. Then the trail crosses along the bottom of a clear-cut and climbs to a view. The high, serrated ridge on the right is Mt. Lafayette; the more rounded peak on the left is Mt. Garfield. Go back down the line of trees, presumably left standing to provide a surface for the blue diamond markers.

Turn right on the trail you came in on, and then immediately left for the parking lot.

Badger Loop

Start as for the Beaver Trail. At the junction, the Badger Trail climbs, winding back and forth across skid roads, before dropping to a bridge and continuing upward to the junction with the Moose Watch Trail.

Where the Moose Watch Trail climbs steeply to the right, the Badger Trail diverges left with a slight upgrade, then turns and starts its downward drop. The steep downgrades have a fair run-out and are broken by short, flatter spots. Lower down there are a couple of short, steep upgrades.

From the junction with the return loop of the Moose Watch Trail, the last quarter mile starts gently upward and crosses a clear-cut with Mts. Lafayette and Garfield standing boldly against the sky. The woods beyond are rocky, wet, hold snow poorly, and have traffic from both trails. But you are nearly back to the end of the loop. Turn right at the junction where you came in, to reach the parking lot.

Moose Watch Loop

The downgrades on this trail are, if anything, less steep than the Badger Loop, except for three short awkward spots along the return traverse. The Moose Watch Loop's difficulty lies in its substantially greater distance, its steep uphill, its exposure to the northwest wind, and its long up-grade for the final mile. On the plus side, the views of the surrounding mountains are seen from unusual angles.

Start on the Beaver Trail, then follow the Badger Trail to the next junction. If you are tired when you reach this junction, take the Badger Trail. You are less than half the climb and a quarter of the distance on the Moose Watch Loop.

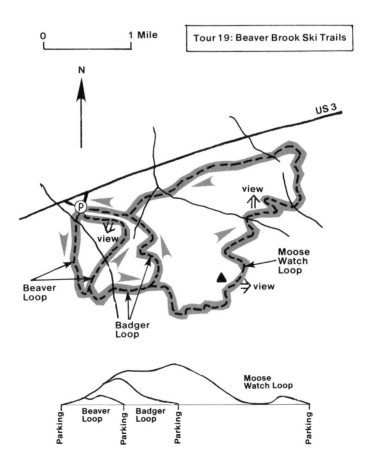

Where the Badger Loop turns left, the Moose Watch Loop climbs substantially along a wet area, swings south on a gentler traverse, and climbs steeply again up a ramp lined with large boulders. It then snakes less steeply back and forth past a large birch/small spruce forest, the type typically found at lower elevations in the White Mountains.

Near the top of the hill a clear-cut area provides a good view east, which is best seen by walking out into the open. The steep little bump in the foreground is the Haystack. The large mountain to the southeast is South Twin, the small mountains to the east are the Sugarloaves.

This clear-cut area is a reminder that in the early 1900s the fashion in logging was to cut everything and scram, leaving desolation and flooding behind—not to mention forest fires, which were fed by the dry slash. Later the fashion was selective cutting, in which only a few of the best trees are taken, and the area is re-cut later, giving a sustained yield. This is esthetically pleasing, as there are always trees, but it also has disadvantages. Selective cutting is more difficult and expensive; trash trees must also be removed. Some trees grow better, or only, in sun or shade, which limits the type of trees best grown. Selective cutting is still the way to grow hemlock and beech.

As with everything else, the fashion has changed again— this time to a modified clear-cut. Instead of wiping out whole watersheds, loggers cut only a small area at once, and trees are left near streams and ponds. The best trees go for saw-logs, others for pulp, and all the small branches that used to be left on the ground to dry out and become a fire hazard go through the shredder and become fiberboard or bioenergy pellets. In 70 years the area can be cut again, while other areas can be cut in their turn. Meanwhile the open areas are good for the deer and other wildlife.

This clear-cut area is the highest point on the trip. A moderate downgrade leads to the top of another clear-cut with views north. The trail continues cutting back and forth along the east side of the opening until its last, steep drop at the northeast end.

The western leg climbs gently, sometimes moderately, with some rough going among rocks and over bridged brooks. On this trail, a good snow cover is a big asset. Two more difficult spots drop steeply with poor run-out and are followed by a steep climb. Tracks show that most people sidestep them, at least partway, on both sides. After the third climb, the trail levels off and comes to the junction with the return loop of the Badger Trail, which it follows back to the loop junction. The parking lot is to the right.

Sometimes food is the best part of the day.

Distance: 3.6 miles one way
Difficulty: minimal/easy
Surface: old logging road
Maps: AMC Mt. Washington, DeLorme, USFS Androscoggin

In 1847, Hayes Copp was the pioneer settler of the area at the foot of the Great Gulf. His namesake trail has been, and will be again, a loop, but for now the western portion of it is closed for logging until 1990. The eastern section of the trail follows an old logging road at an easy grade, largely coinciding with the old Great Gulf Trail.

The trail leads up the lower part of the Great Gulf, one of the big glacial ravines on Mt. Washington. However, it offers no views of the summits; the first viewpoint, the Bluff, is still a mile beyond the end of the ski trail. It is reached by a steep uphill climb, and even accomplished ski mountaineers find the trip to it very difficult.

The highway offers even better views of the mountains and the ravines. Allow some time in the morning, when the light is better, to stop at one or more of the pull-offs in the vicinity of the Mt. Washington Auto Road for the view. Stop again on the way home to see the summits in a different light.

Driving Directions
Dolly Copp Campground, named for Hayes Copp's wife, is off NH-16 on the west side, 4.5 miles south of Gorham and 3.4 miles north of the Auto Road at Glen House. An area is plowed for parking.

Hayes Copp Ski Trail
The ski trail follows the road south from the information sign. Look left across the picnic area to see the Imp Profile

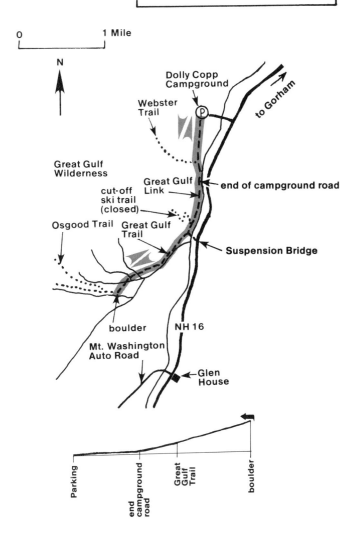

on the right side of a small knoll on the far side of the valley. The Imp is a byproduct of the glacier that slid up the near side of the mountains, smoothed them off, and then broke off chunks on the downslope side, leaving the reverse slope more jagged. The Daniel Webster Scout Trail leads right to Mt. Madison.

At the end of the campground road, the Hayes Copp Ski Trail continues on the Great Gulf Link, marked by blue plastic diamonds. Pass a cut-off ski trail to the western loop (closed for logging). In three-quarters of a mile a trail leads left to the new hiker access that replaced the lower part of the Osgood Trail. The suspension bridge over the Peabody River is an attraction for bridge buffs, but it is not easy to reach on skis.

Continue now on the Great Gulf Trail, right. Farther on, it diverges left to follow the stream more closely, while the ski trail continues on the logging road. After they rejoin, skiers must negotiate three bridges that cross small dips. Because the bridges thaw and freeze before the ski surface, there may be a noticeable drop from the trail. This presents a small problem on the ascent, but more on the descent. The last one returning is the most difficult—watch for it.

The trail then passes through a mature deciduous forest with many large birch trees. Note the small, shade-loving conifers coming up underneath.

The Hayes Copp Ski Trail currently ends at the Great Gulf Wilderness boundary, and one returns the same way. However, a tenth of a mile farther up the Great Gulf Trail is an immense boulder on the left, which makes a good objective.

Typical Forest Service trail sign.

LOWE'S BALD SPOT

Pinkham Notch, Gorham

	Old Jackson Rd.	Auto Road	Connie's Way
Distance:	1.7 miles	1.5 miles	4.0 miles
	(Total loop trip 7.6 miles)		
Difficulty:	difficult	moderate/easy	difficult
Surface:	hiking trail	graded road	ski trail

Maps: AMC Mt. Washington (not Connie's Way), DeLorme

All of the trails in Pinkham Notch are steep and difficult, and these are no exception. Aside from the thrill of skiing on the lower slopes of Mt. Washington, the major attraction of this trip is reaching the scenic viewpoint at Lowe's Bald Spot.

Any section of this trail may be done as a return trip. Because the hills are less steep, the skiing in the clockwise direction, as described, is substantially easier than the counterclockwise direction. Starting at Glen House (if permitted) would add over a mile in distance and several hundred feet of elevation.

Although snow comes early to the north country, a deep base is required on these trails. The trip is strenuous, and it may be wise to save it for later in the season.

Driving Directions

Nestled at the foot of Mt. Washington, the Appalachian Mountain Club's Pinkham Notch establishment is on the west side of the height-of-land on NH-16 between Jackson and Gorham. You really can't miss it.

This is the north country headquarters of the AMC. The main desk is in the building to the right of the courtyard, where guidebooks, maps, and the latest trail and weather information can be obtained. Public rest rooms are in the

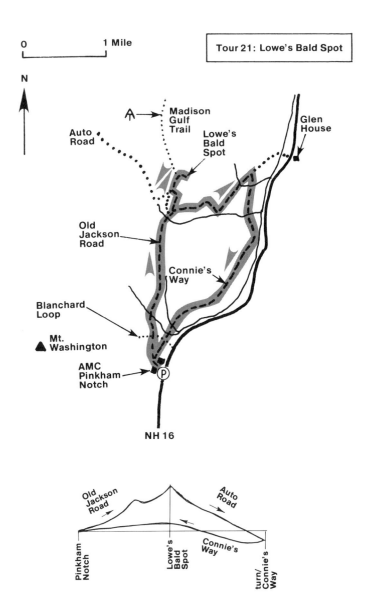

0   1 Mile

N

Tour 21: Lowe's Bald Spot

Madison
Gulf
Trail

Glen
House

Auto
Road

Lowe's
Bald
Spot

Old
Jackson
Road

Connie's
Way

Blanchard
Loop

Mt.
Washington

AMC
Pinkham
Notch

P

NH 16

Old Jackson Road

Auto Road

Connie's Way

Pinkham Notch

Lowe's Bald Spot

turn/Connie's Way

basement of the building. Accommodations and meals are available by reservation.

Old Jackson Road

Bear right behind the main building on the Tuckerman Ravine Trail, and immediately right again on Old Jackson Road (OJR). It was built in 1885 as a short cut to the Auto Road from the south. The present trail has been substantially relocated in the steeper places to bypass eroded and wet spots.

The Appalachian Trail follows the OJR nearly to the Auto Road, so it is blazed with white-painted vertical rectangles. If the sun is out, and prevailing wind from the northwest, dress lightly to start, but carry sufficient warm layers or you will freeze at lunch.

The trail climbs gently to Blanchard Loop (you will return here) and other ski trails. Climb steeply to the notch between the little cliff-like ridge on the right seen from Pinkham and the lower slopes of Nelson Crag. While circling on the sidehill, frequent small brooks are crossed. The trail then levels off a bit through the notch before dropping and climbing again to a brook crossing. Here the hiking trail takes a sharp left to avoid the short road walk to the Madison Gulf Trail. Skiers continue straight ahead to the Auto Road. Replace your layers as needed.

Lowe's Bald Spot

To visit Lowe's Bald Spot, the knob seen straight ahead, turn left on the Auto Road. Pass the two-mile mark, and where the road switches sharply back left, turn right on the Madison Gulf Trail. The blue-blazed trail soon bears right. You may want to remove your skis for the steep climb up the ledges, which is difficult, but short.

Although the summits of Mts. Washington and Jefferson are obscured by the nearer ridge, Mts. Adams and Madison are seen on the right, Boott Spur on the left, and across the valley, the ski area on Wildcat Mountain.

Auto Road

Continue downhill on the road from the junction with Madison Gulf Trail; the surface may be rough from tracked vehicles. The drop is steady, but less steep farther down. Just past the one-mile mark is the WMNF Boundary sign on the right, a large gravel pit on the left, and a view of the Glen House area down in the valley. The turn on Connie's Way is downhill as far as you see on the road. Turn right at the outside of a left-hand turn on the Auto Road.

Cliffs decorated with ice frosting.

Connie's Way

Not only is the turn to Connie's Way lower in elevation than Pinkham, but it also climbs up and down over the end of the ridge. (Walking back on NH-16 is easier, and leaving a car there is easiest yet.)

On Connie's Way, occasionally marked by the customary blue diamonds, all large streams are bridged. The mountains shelter it from the north and west winds.

The trail crosses a stream, cuts back right, and climbs over a ridge. The next bridge has a short, steep sidehill on the far side, to the ridge. Circle right through a minor col and climb the next ridge. Near the high point are large boulders on the right. (This may remind you of knitting directions: *(drop, cross stream, circle, climb over ridge) Repeat from * X number of times.)

When you come to the tiny pond on the right, it is mostly level or downhill the rest of the way. Cross a wet area and a number of small streams, then at Blanchard Loop, one-half mile from Pinkham—turn right, then left and left again on OJR.

If you signed out, don't forget to sign back in.

Additional Skiing

Several other ski trails have been built in the area, but none is really easy. Ask for the map at Pinkham.

It is possible to ski up the Auto Road farther. The usual objective is a viewpoint shortly above the former Halfway House, near the 4-mile mark. Do not venture higher on the mountain unless conditions are good and you are well equipped and really know what you are doing. Too many people have been lured up only to be caught short by a sudden change of weather.

View of Mts. Adams and Madison from Lowe's Bald Spot.

MOUNTAIN POND

	Road	**Trail**
Distance:	3.2 miles one way	0.3 mile to pond; + 0.6 mile to shelter
	(Total round trip to shelter 8.2 miles)	
Difficulty:	minimal	moderate
Surface:	graded road	trail

Maps: AMC Carter Mahoosuc, DeLorme

Mountain Pond is a wild pond three-quarters of a mile long and a quarter mile wide, lying at the south end of the Bald-face Ridge. Most of the trip is on the unplowed Slippery Brook Road. Heavy snowmobile traffic breaks up the icy crust and packs down the heavy snow; this is a place to go when conditions are terrible. The road is wide enough to accommodate various types of winter recreationists; the pond is less frequented.

Driving Directions

From North Conway, take US-302/NH-16 north from the rest area north of town 2.2 miles. Turn east on Town Hall Road. For people coming the other direction, this turn is 1.6 miles southeast of Glen (junction US-302/NH-16).

Cross the Intervale Loop road and continue ahead 3.3 miles to a plowed parking area.

Mountain Pond

The Slippery Brook Road, FR-17, is a wide, graded road, open to ordinary traffic in the summer. Except for one downgrade near the start, the road trends gently upward, often within sight of the East Branch of the Saco River. The East Branch Trail is on the left at nearly two-and-a-half miles, and later the East Branch Road, FR-38, diverges left, carrying the snowmobile trail to Wild River. Keep right, climbing a little more steeply at the start, for three-quarters of a mile to the trail to Mountain Pond on the right.

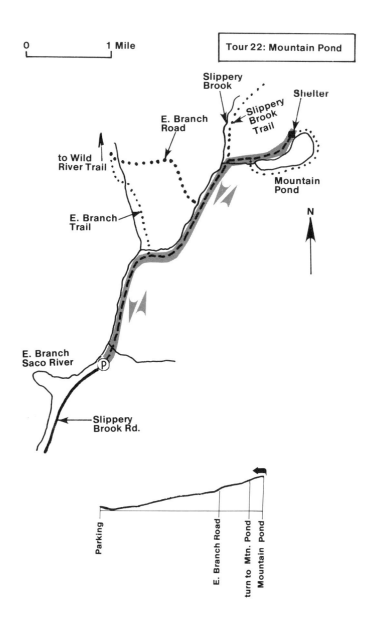

0   1 Mile

Tour 22: Mountain Pond

Slippery
Brook

Slippery
Brook
Trail

Shelter

E. Branch
Road

to Wild
River Trail

Mountain
Pond

E. Branch
Trail

N

E. Branch
Saco River

P

Slippery
Brook Rd.

Parking

E. Branch Road

turn to Mtn. Pond

Mountain Pond

The going here is narrow and a little steep in places, but it's less than a half mile to the junction with the loop trail around the pond. Bear left to the shore of the pond at the outlet brook and the shelter another half mile away on the north shore.

At this point you need to decide if you should take the easier and more scenic route across the ice, or the safer and more difficult trail along the shore. Some people cross ice all the time with no problem. Some people fall through the ice with little or no problem. Some people fall through the ice and have a serious or fatal problem. Other people never go near ice at all.

If there is a *fresh* snowmobile track, I feel it's safe to ski on it. If the ice is bare, or lightly covered, looks good, and the weather has been cold, it is probably safe. If the lake has a heavy coating of fresh snow, especially following a warm spell, there is no telling what it may conceal. I crossed this pond once after a heavy snowfall, the last of a party of three. Out in the middle I went through the snow and an upper layer of thin ice into a patch of slush. Fortunately it was on top of a thicker layer of ice, so I was wet only to the instep. Drying and rewaxing my skis took a while.

Staying close to the shore may seem safer, but the ice here is more apt to have soft spots particularly near inlet streams or over springs. Also, ice melts first along the shore in the spring.

If you plan to cross ice, plan your rescue in advance. Spread out the party to reduce weight and insure everyone doesn't go in together. If you don't have a rope, ski poles may be looped together to make an extension pole.

Additional Skiing
A hiking trail circles the pond. In addition, both the Slippery Brook Trail and the East Branch Trail go on for miles; ski as

far on either as you wish and return. Both cross a height-of-land before coming out on NH/ME 113 in the Evans Notch area.

Should you be fortunate enough to be spending the night in the area, either at the shelter, or in a ski cabin as I was, be sure to have a look at the stars if the night is clear. If you study a star chart inside, rather than by flash light outside, you not only reduce the time spent out in the cold but also preserve your night vision, allowing you to see the less bright stars more clearly. The time it takes eyes to adjust from bright light to dark varies with the individual, but may be as much as fifteen minutes.

A Forest Service Adirondack lean-to.

ROCKY BRANCH TRAIL

	Road	**Trail**
Distance:	2 miles one way	2 miles one way
		(Total round trip 8 miles)
Difficulty:	minimal	easy
Surface:	graded road	eroded RR bed

Maps: AMC Mt. Washington, DeLorme

The Rocky Branch trail is easy, following a Forest Service fire road and an old railroad grade. Another skier asked me, "Does this trip make a nice run?" Answer: "No, but it makes a nice walk."

Driving Directions

The Jericho Road leaves US-302 just east of the bridge over Rocky Branch, which is 1 mile west of Glen (junction US-302/NH-16) and 5.5 miles east of the blinking light in Bartlett. Drive 3 miles up the road, which becomes FR-27, to the plowed parking area.

Rocky Branch Trail

Ski along the road, downhill at first, then gently uphill. At just under two miles the road is gated at a bridge over the Rocky Branch. The fire road continues on the other side another quarter mile.

From the bridge, the Rocky Branch Trail follows the old railroad bed all the way. This was one of the last White Mountain railroads, operating from 1908 until 1914. It ceased operations early due to three bad fires.

The railroad ran all the way up the valley beyond Mt. Isolation, crossing the river seven times on trestles, all of which are now missing. Engine Hill, where the gradient increases to 12%, was allegedly named for one of the many railroad accidents. The runaway engine derailed, but the crew was able to jump to safety.

One unique feature of the logging in this area was the use of a horse and cable hoist to bring logs uphill over the watershed divide at Maple Hill rather than building a spur line.

The tree-lined railroad grade runs straight ahead, the only problem being an occasional trickle of water that erodes a dip across the road. A mile in, a trestle is missing, and the

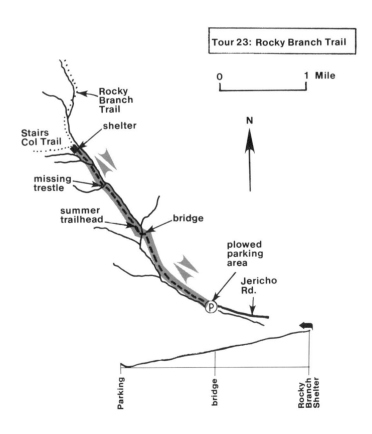

trail climbs gently up a little ridge and down the other side. The Rocky Branch is occasionally in sight on the right.

Another slightly larger, but still small, stream may be crossed on the ice. When the Giant Stairs appear on the skyline around the shoulder of Mt. Resolution, you are nearly there. The trail to Rocky Branch Shelter #1 is on the right, almost opposite the Stairs Col Trail on the left.

You can continue up the Rocky Branch Trail until the stream crossings or the gradient become too difficult.

Crossing a frozen brook; old railroad grade in the background.

WILLARD NOTCH

Lancaster, Kilkenny

Distance: 5 miles one way
Difficulty: minimal/moderate last 2 miles
Surface: graded road, eroded logging road

Map: AMC Pilot

Although this trip lies the farthest north, I wouldn't call it a true wilderness experience. Instead, it is a congenial sharing of a lovely area with snowmobiles, loggers, campers, and others. The first three miles of the trail are on easy roads, the last climb to the notch is steeper and quite eroded.

Driving Directions

From US-2 in Jefferson, take North Road, which is 0.1 mile west of the junction with NH-116. Go north 2.3 miles, turn right on Gore Road. At 1.5 miles bear left. In 0.3 mile turn right on Pleasant Valley Road, and right again in 0.7 mile on Art White Road. This road is gated at 0.5 mile, with a parking area on the left.

York Pond Trail

Go through the gate and up the road, following the Forest Service signs. This area has recently been clear-cut, which opened up mountain views in all directions. Mt. Cabot is to the left, the Weeks Mts. are straight ahead, and Mt. Waumbek is to the right. (When a section like this has been clear-cut, the birch trees are left standing in order to reseed the area, as birch is a valuable tree to grow.)

In a half mile, at a crossroad at the edge of the clearing, the Mt. Cabot Trail goes on ahead, while the York Pond Trail takes the right along the edge of the woods. Turn here. The trail then enters the woods through an arcade of spruces, crosses another road, and comes out on a traveled road a half mile from the turn. Bear left. (This turn is easy to miss on the return.)

There are a number of small cottages and a log yard along this road, but past them, the road becomes less well used. A mile from the start, the trail enters the National Forest. The boundary sign is on the left side of the road, with the marked Witness Trees adding to its visibility. The adjacent

Clear-cut opens mountain views; birch trees left for reseeding.

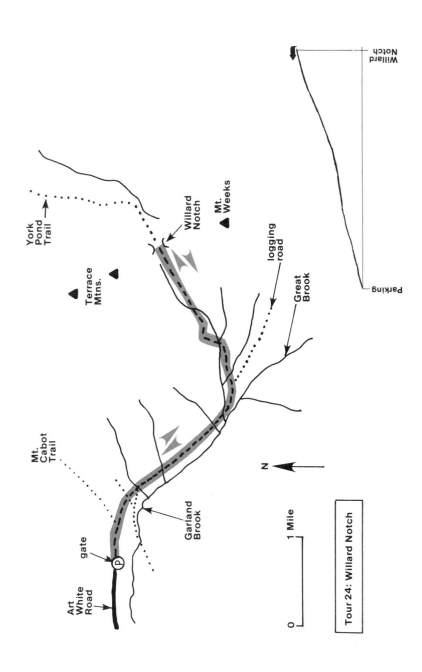

York Pond Trail

Willard Notch

Mt. Weeks

Terrace Mtns.

logging road

Great Brook

Mt. Cabot Trail

Garland Brook

gate

Art White Road

N

1 Mile

0

Tour 24: Willard Notch

Willard Notch

Parking

trees of an important boundary, in this case between public and private land, are often marked with paint, or in this case with metal signs. The road continues level or drops slightly along the bed of an old logging railroad.

Much of the middle part of the trip follows the bed of the Kilkenny Railroad, which ran from Coos Junction, near Lancaster, to the forks of Garland Brook. The logging railroads were built starting in the northern White Mountains, and moving south later, probably because there was a main line from Portland that ran north of the mountains. This was one of the earlier roads and ran only in the winter. This made for a considerable savings, because the frost in the ground could be used to stabilize the road bed instead of expensive fill. Also, engines used in summer for excursions could be rented fairly cheaply.

Three miles from the start is a major brook crossing. It is not bridged, but in ski season the ice usually provides a good crossing.

The trail starts to climb now at a moderate rate, and the difficulty increases. In half a mile a logging road goes ahead; the trail leads left, downhill across a gully. It climbs gradually along the south side of the notch, up and down, to its high point. The cliffs of East Terrace Mountain stand out to the north, and North Weeks is to the south.

Where the trail starts to drop off steeply, to York Pond on the far side, it is time to turn around and return.

ZEALAND VALLEY

	Zealand Road	Spruce Goose	Zealand Trail
Distance:	3.5 miles one way	4.1 miles one way	2.5 miles one way
Difficulty:	minimal/easy	moderate/difficult	easy/moderate
Surface:	road	ski trail	RR bed/hiking trail

Maps: AMC Franconia, DeLorme

This is a classic ski trip, partially on an old railroad bed, leading to a deep scenic notch. An AMC Hut, open in the winter, is accessible via this route. The summer road running 3.5 miles up the valley is gated. Snowmobile and ski trails have been built parallel to the road on opposite sides, to provide for recreational use when it is plowed for logging operations.

The Zealand Valley has undergone several transformations, from "clear-cut and get out," to devastation in the early 1900s by fire and flood, to an example of the recuperative power of nature. Forest fires are always a problem in the woods, and the dry slash left from logging is frequently tinder dry. In 1886 a spark from a wood-burning locomotive caused a major fire that covered the entire valley. Not only does fire destroy the vegetation itself, but the lack of tree roots reduces the water-holding power of the soil, contributing to fast run-off of ground water after rains and erosion in general. The weakening of the bonding of soil on steep slopes creates the condition for landslides, which destroys the soil down to the bedrock. Whitewall Mountain, to the left of the Notch, as seen from the north, is an example of this.

From the end of the Forest Service road, most of the better going on the Zealand Trail is on the old railroad bed. The rougher sections usually occur where the railroad crossed the Zealand River and the trail does not. One of the best places to see the railroad bed is at the start. The line continued through Zealand Notch along the side of White-wall Mountain—where it has been damaged by slides—to Ethan and Shoal ponds. The engine backed up the notch with the cars above, so the strain was not on the couplings, and a turn-around was not required at the top.

It makes an intriguing historical note to recall that back in the days when the only through New Hampshire railroad skirted the western edge of the state along the Connecticut and Ammonoosuc Rivers, the Zealand Railroad had a charter to join with any other railroad in the state to provide a north-south route. It never exercised this privilege, though, as it was nearly out of business by the time tracks came north from Concord, up the East Branch of the Pemigewasset River. Imagine if these railroads had driven their golden spike near Thoreau Falls. What is now the Pemigewasset Wilderness would have become the main line instead of Crawford Notch. The engineering would have been no more difficult—perhaps easier.

The mill near the present site of the Zealand Campground burned in 1897; operations were already pretty well over by the time of the fires of 1903. The land was sold to the Forest Service in 1915.

Driving Directions

The Zealand Road leaves south from US-302 at the Zealand Campground, located 2.3 miles east of US-3 in Twin Mountain and 2.3 miles west of Fabyan.

No parking here! The parking area is a quarter mile east on the other side of US-302. The underpass is at the extreme east end of the parking area.

Zealand Road

Cross the bridge over the Ammonoosuc River at Zealand Campround. The snowmobile trail leaves left immediately,

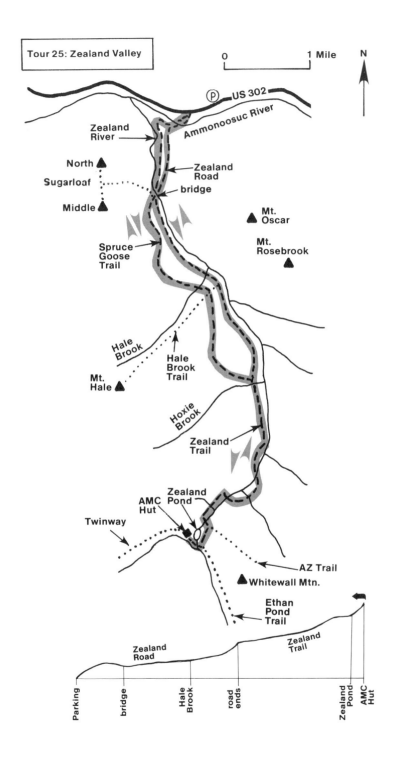

Tour 25: Zealand Valley

but the Spruce Goose Ski Trail turns right at the top of the first rise.

The road climbs steeply for nearly a mile, leveling off by the campground and crossing the bridge over the Zealand River. The next couple of miles are so level that skis won't glide on the return. Double poling may be advised. The river is briefly in sight on the left. Pass Hale Brook Trail on the right at two and a half miles, and a logging road on the left at the start of the last short steep hill to the parking lot, where the road ends at 3.5 miles.

Spruce Goose Ski Trail

The ski trail is a half mile longer than the road and substantially more difficult. A profile is not given, as it would be similar to the road, a hundred feet or so higher. The minor ups and downs which make it so much harder won't show at this scale.

Cross the Ammonoosuc River on the Zealand Road Bridge. The Spruce Goose Ski Trail turns right at the top of the first grade. It alternates steep climbs with rolling ups and downs. Starting parallel to the road it circles the lower campground and climbs to the road at the upper campground. Turn right and follow the road south along the top of the hill, again turning right where it bears left. Drop slightly to the bridge over the Zealand River where all routes converge.

Do not take the hiking trail to Mt. Sugarloaf! Where the snowmobile trail takes a sharp right, bear right slightly onto the ski trail, which parallels the road. While this road is virtually level and graded, the ski trail climbs high, up and down over brooks, often within sight of the road below.

On the Rosebrook Range across the valley, the first ledgy summit is Mt. Oscar. Pointed Mt. Rosebrook is opposite the Hale Brook Trail, and the last summit south is Mt. Tom.

Several snowmobile trails and logging roads cross. Be forewarned—Twin Mountain is snowmobile country, and skiers are not welcome on their trails.

All streams have bridges that are easy to cross, but some of the grades over the minor ridges are steep. Where the road is again in sight briefly, the Hale Brook Trail crosses, usually identifiable because of the tracks on it. The ski trail swings away from the road and continues its undulating progress, trending steeply uphill. It reaches the Zealand Road at the south end of the parking lot just before the bridge.

Helping a fallen skier up.

Zealand Trail

This trail follows the old railroad grade at the start, climbs over the hillside to the right with a little rough going among some rocks, and falls back to the railroad grade. A scenic spot on the Zealand River at some ledges is less than a mile from the parking lot. The trail crosses back and forth across the valley and streams, with all but one crossing bridged.

The bridges are not an unmixed blessing, though, as they were designed for hikers and not skiers. Most of them have rock steps leading up and down, which are difficult to negotiate on skis, particularly when snow conditions are bad. Where the trail crosses back across a swamp (courtesy of beavers) to the west side of the valley at around two miles, the low log bridges often have washed out of position in the high water, and during winter thaws the ice may not be strong enough to cross. Use care. Beyond the junction with the AZ trail at almost two and a half miles, the trail passes to the east of Zealand Pond to the trail junction at the south end. Across the pond, Zealand Hut can be seen high up beside the waterfall to the west.*

Zealand Hut

From the trail junction at the south end of the pond it is one fifth of a mile to the hut. The Twinway crosses the south outlet of the pond on puncheon; you may prefer an alternate route—follow the tracks. The trail climbs steeply up to the hut, and people often leave their skis at the bottom.

The view from the hut through Zealand Notch to Carrigain Notch is outstanding.

---

*Note: A new ski-touring trail is being cut from the end of the road to Zealand Hut; the bridges are being rebuilt in the fall of 1988.

Zealand Hut is one of the AMC's mountain hiking huts, offering beds and meals in the summer. It is one of two open in the winter, but the caretaker does not provide food service or blankets. There is no running water, minimal heat, and little chance to dry wet things. Triple decker bunks with mattresses are available, but there is no heat in the bunk rooms. Bring your own sleeping bag and food. Current rates and reservations are available from AMC Pinkham.

In the summer Zealand is one of the most accessible huts. In the winter the round trip is twelve and a half miles via the road and thirteen and a half via the ski trail. It is a very long day, and most campers unused to skiing with an overnight pack vastly underestimate the time needed to reach the hut.

Additional Skiing

Views of Zealand Notch from the old railroad grade along the side of Whitewall Mountain are easily reached via the Ethan Pond Trail. Energetic skiers spend much time planning through trips to Crawford Notch via the Ethan Pond Trail or the Kancamagus Highway via the Wilderness Trail. Few of them actually attempt the trip, and a goodly number of those who do, sincerely wish they hadn't.

However, persons staying at the hut can find many miles of trail to ski while they are there.

CROSS-COUNTRY SKI AREAS ASSOCIATION

Balsams/Wilderness
Dixville Notch, 03576
603-255-3400

Bretton Woods Ski-Touring Area
Route 302
Bretton Woods, 03575
603-278-5181

Gulf Brook Nordic Center
P.O. Box 95
Danbury, 03230
603-768-3600

Gunstock X-Country Center
Rt. 11A
Gilford, 03247
603-293-4341

Inn at East Hill Farm
Mountain Road
Troy, 03465
603-242-6495

Jackson Ski-Touring Foundation
Main St., P.O. Box 216
Jackson, 03946
603-383-9355

Loon Mountain
Lincoln, 03251
603-745-8111

Norsk Sports
RR 2, Box 735
New London, 03257
603-526-4685

Quaker Hollow Farm
14 Huntington Road
Henniker, 03242
603-428-7639

River Bend
171 Central Street
Woodsville, 03785
603-747-3581

Sargent Touring Center—BU
RFD 2M, Windy Row
Peterborough, 03459
603-525-3311

Shattuck Inn Nordic Center
28 Dublin Road
Jaffrey Center, 03454
603-532-6619

Temple Mountain Ski Area
P.O. Box 368, Route 101
Peterborough, 03458
603-924-9376

The Nordic Skier XC Ski Center
19 North Main Street
Wolfeboro, 03894
603-569-3151

Waterville Valley Ski Area
Waterville Valley, 03215
603-236-4666

Windblown
Route 124, Box 669
New Ipswich, 03071
603-878-2869

GUIDEBOOKS FROM THE COUNTRYMAN PRESS AND BACKCOUNTRY PUBLICATIONS

• •

Written for people of all ages and experience, these popular and carefully prepared books feature detailed trail and tour directions, notes on points of interest and natural phenomena, maps and photographs.

Walks and Rambles Series

Walks and Rambles on the Delmarva Peninsula, $8.95
Walks and Rambles in Westchester (NY) and Fairfield (CT) Counties, $7.95
Walks and Rambles in Rhode Island, $8.95

Biking Series

25 Bicycle Tours in New Jersey, $8.95
25 Bicycle Tours on Delmarva, $8.95
25 Bicycle Tours in Maine, $8.95
25 Bicycle Tours in Vermont, $8.95
25 Bicycle Tours in New Hampshire, $6.95
20 Bicycle Tours in the Finger Lakes, $7.95
20 Bicycle Tours in and around New York City, $7.95
25 Bicycle Tours in Eastern Pennsylvania, $7.95

Canoeing Series

Canoe Camping Vermont and New Hampshire Rivers, $7.95
Canoeing Central New York, $9.95
Canoeing Massachusetts, Rhode Island and Connecticut, $7.95

Hiking Series

50 Hikes in New Jersey, $10.95
50 Hikes in the Adirondacks, $10.95
50 Hikes in Central New York, $8.95
50 Hikes in the Hudson Valley, $9.95
50 Hikes in Central Pennsylvania, $9.95
50 Hikes in Eastern Pennsylvania, $9.95
50 Hikes in Western Pennsylvania, $9.95
50 Hikes in Maine, $8.95
50 Hikes in the White Mountains, $9.95

50 More Hikes in New Hampshire, $9.95
50 Hikes in Vermont, 3rd edition, $9.95
50 Hikes in Massachusetts, $9.95
50 Hikes in Connecticut, $8.95
50 Hikes in West Virginia, $9.95

Adirondack Series

Discover the Southern Adirondacks $9.95
Discover the South Central Adirondacks $8.95
Discover the Southeastern Adirondacks $8.95
Discover the Central Adirondacks $8.95
Discover the Southwestern Adirondacks $9.95
Discover the Northeastern Adirondacks $9.95
Discover the Eastern Adirondacks $9.95
Discover the West Central Adirondacks $13.95
Discover the Northern Adirondacks $10.95

Ski-Touring Series

25 Ski Tours in Central New York $7.95
25 Ski Tours in the Adirondacks $5.95
25 Ski Tours in Eastern Massachusetts $7.95
25 Ski Tours in New Hampshire $8.95

Other Guides

State Parks and Campgrounds in Northern New York $9.95
The Other Massachusetts: An Explorer's Guide $12.95
Maine: An Explorer's Guide (revised edition available spring 1989)
Vermont: An Explorer's Guide, 3rd edition, $14.95
New England's Special Places $10.95
New York's Special Places, $12.95

The above titles are available at bookstores and at certain sporting goods stores or may be ordered directly from the publisher. For complete descriptions of these and other guides, write: The Countryman Press, P.O. Box 175, Woodstock, VT 05091.